ZODIAC

BALLYMENA

Edited by Steve Twelvetree

First published in Great Britain in 2002 by
YOUNG WRITERS
Remus House,
Coltsfoot Drive,
Peterborough, PE2 9JX
Telephone (01733) 890066

All Rights Reserved

Copyright Contributors 2002

HB ISBN 0 75433 534 8
SB ISBN 0 75433 535 6

FOREWORD

Young Writers was established in 1991 with the aim of promoting creative writing in children, to make reading and writing poetry fun.

Once again, this year proved to be a tremendous success with over 41,000 entries received nationwide.

The Zodiac competition has shown us the high standard of work and effort that children are capable of today. The competition has given us a vivid insight into the thoughts and experiences of today's younger generation. It is a reflection of the enthusiasm and creativity that teachers have injected into their pupils, and it shines clearly within this anthology.

The task of selecting poems was a difficult one, but nevertheless, an enjoyable experience. We hope you are as pleased with the final selection in *Zodiac Ballymena* as we are.

CONTENTS

Ballee High School
- Gemma Gilmore — 1
- Gemma Greenwood — 2
- Laura-Lee Kane — 2
- Jamie McKay — 3
- Kylie Magill — 4
- Dana Curtis — 4
- Musharat Nara — 5

Ballymena Academy
- Samuel Steele — 5
- Rachel Hamilton — 6
- Philip Coulter — 6
- Alison Beattie — 7
- Sarah Bell — 8
- David Manson — 8
- Peter Coulter — 9
- Grace McBurney — 10
- David McCooke — 10
- Claire Ferguson — 11
- Cheryl Gaston — 12
- Amanda Milligan — 12
- Laura Sherrey — 13
- Kathryn Shaw — 14
- Jason Dalrymple — 14
- Angela Telford — 15
- Charlotte Knowles — 16
- James Erwin — 17
- Richard Gilmore — 18
- Sarah Pedlow — 18
- Heather Darby — 19
- Timothy Bamber — 20
- Louise Stirling — 21
- Ben Kennedy — 22

Alan Norton	22
Andrew Robinson	23
Stephen Donaldson	23
Catherine Lynn	24
Lynne McCosh	25
Joel Hutchinson	26
Alex Loxley	27
Alison Young	28
Mark Kerr	28
Emma Boyd	29
Steven Carson	30
Rachael Laughlin	31
Lyndsey Hamill	32
Stephanie McKervill	33
Suzanne Smyth	34
John Carson	35
Alan Scroggie	36
Andrew Scott	36
Laura McKelvey	37
Rachel Rainey	38
David McCrory	39
Ashley Craig	40
Lauren Houston	41
Ryan Walker	42
Richard Ross	43
Christine McBurney	44
Victoria Murdock	45
Inès Delpy	46
Rebecca Knowles	47
Rachel Heaney	48
Steven Kernoham	49
Neil Paul	50
Nicole McBurney	50
Roddy Montgomery	51
Adam Brady	51
Jenny Marshall	52
Paul Lamont	53

Andrew Shields	54
Kirsty Robinson	54
Judy McAllister	55
David Frew	56
Jonathan Jackson	56
Jenna Fletcher	57
Fergus Roulston	58
Emma Wilkinson	58
David Gault	59
Jamie Anne Wallace	60
Rachael Ramsey	61
David McMaster	62
Jonathan Mark	62
Alan Clarke	63
Matthew Young	64
Richard Wallace	65
Kerry Aiken	66
Laura Featherstone	67
Jonathon Waddell	68
Deborah McGuckin	69
Sharon Davison	70
Lorraine Fleming	70
Alex Megarry	71
Kathy Michael	72
Alison Moore	72
Patrick Harper	73
Myles Hanna	74
Andrew Moore	74
Nathan Hodge	75
Charis McNabney	76
Sarah Kernohan	77
Jonathan McLean	78
Russell Kerr	79
Brian Millar	80
Louise McGivern	81
Garrett T Bell	82
William Fleck	82

Katie D'Arcy	83
Rebecca Sweetlove	83
Jenny Surgenor	84
Philip Harshaw	85
James Bond	86
Clare Bamber	86
Adam Bond	87
Craig Barr	88
Hannah J Simms	88
Clare Kennedy	89
Coral Gardner	90
Robin Adair	90
Jenny Patton	91
Erin Russell	92
Amy Colgan	92
Timothy Rocks	93
David McComb	93
Kristine Porter	94
Rachel Swann	95
Emma Logan	96
Rory Smith	97
Aisling Dundee	98
Rebecca Stevenson	98
Dale Gallagher	99
John Gregg	100
Rebecca Dempster	101
Shwetha Janarthanan	102
Craig Edwards	102
Joanne Healy	103
Jonathan Davison	104
Adam Gault	104
Christopher Patton	105
Ben McQueen	106
Alistair Black	107
Adam Shingleton	108
Nikita Strange	109
Diane Wilson	110

Matthew Wilson	111
Alan Graham	112
Alison Craig	113
Carole Addis	114
Andrea McGuigan	115

Cambridge House Grammar School

Stewart McKee	116
Karine Carleton	116
Ashley King	117
Kathryn McNeilly	117
Davita Duff	118
Michael Steele	118
Gillian Rainey	119
David Stewart	120
Gillian Millar	120
Daniel Cummings	121
Leanne Kernohan	122
Jenna Maxwell	122
Adrian Nicholl	123
David Meeke	124
David Torbitt	124
Simon Jamieson	125
Gareth Marcus	126
Mark McLean	126
Daena Lipsett	127
Ross McKervill	127
Deborah Storey	128
Kristopher Orr	128
Lindsay Forsythe	129
Glenn McGivern	129
Andrew Thompson	130
Gary Pollock	131
Lauren Tennant	131
Andrew Lindsay	132
Simone Forgrave	132
Peter Kennoway	133
Steven Boyce	134

Jason Steele	134
Gary Crawford	135
Michael McMaster	136
David O'Neill	137
Rachel McLaughlin	138
Hugh King	138
Shane McMullan	139
Judith Erwin	139
Jayne McGrillen	140
Nicola McMaster	140
Robert Winton	141
Andrew Colvin	142
Samuel Strange	142
Paul Dunlop	143
Rachel Henry	143
Lynsey McFetridge	144
Jennifer Rock	144
Sarah Rainey	145
Danielle Kinney	146
Laura Livingstone	146
Deborah McCracken	147
Richard Patton	148
Rebecca Mawhinney	148
Rachael Selwood	149
Jason Stewart	149
Jonathan Boyd	150
Lyndsay Williamson	150
Kathy McCarte	151
Rebecca Hanna	152
Megan McCaughan	152
Ruth Barr	153
Ricky Hood	154
Selina Shingleton	155
Victoria McCartney	155
Katy McAllister	156
Vanessa Wilson	156
David Millar	157
Lyndsey Montgomery	158

Kathryn Young	158
Emma Bamber	159
Naomi Millar	160
Nicola Gillespie	160
Pamela Livingstone	161
Carolyn Adams	161
Gayle Armstrong	162
Katie Crooks	162
Kelly Anderton	163
Lauren McMaster	163
Jim Caldwell	164
William McKee	165
Alison Millar	166
Patricia Boyd	166
William Wilson	167
Alison Arnold	168
Amanda Gaston	168
Helyn Rankin	169
Ruth Knowles	169
Julie Whann	170
Sarah Robinson	170
Sarah-Kate Goodwin	171
Paula Kerr	172
Linda McCord	172
Nicola McFall	173
Lucy McGaughey	174
Louise Penny	174
Michaela Beattie	175
Alyson O'Flaherty	175
Selina Thompson	176
Lyndsey Johnston	177
Lauren Rock	177
Laura Kenny	178
Kelly Orr	178
Sharon Reid	179
Melissa Gordon	179

Cullybackey High School
- Scott Moore — 180
- Claire Smyth — 181
- Alastair Irvine — 181
- Michael Dickey — 182
- Charlene McFetridge — 182
- David McCaughey — 182
- Janine Crawford — 183

Dunfane School
- Patrick McCloskey — 183

St Louis Grammar School
- Olivia Devlin — 184
- Marcus McCreight — 185
- Clair McAllister — 186

The Poems

STARS, MOON AND SUN

The stars are so bright,
Up, up in the lovely sky;
There are millions and millions of them,
You can't even count them;
I love looking up in the sky at night,
It is so cool looking at them;
I really like it and so do my friends,
If you had a telescope you could look at them;
The stars are so pretty,
Sometimes you can see the stars in the sky.

I love the moon, it is so bright,
The moon is absolutely big and lovely;
Sometimes there is a full moon or half or quarter,
At night-time it glows and you can look at it;
When it is dark it is there and when it is bright it is gone,
It can go behind clouds and come out again;
The moon spins around like a ball,
The colours of the moon are yellow and light blue;
When you go in the car at night the moon moves,
It is lovely to look at if there's nothing to do.

The sun is so bright,
The colours of the sun are orange, red and yellow;
When the sun is out it is lovely and sunny,
I like the sun when it is warm;
The planets spin around the sun,
If you look at the sun it would hurt your eyes;
It is sometimes out on a warm day,
Sometimes the sun isn't out when it's raining;
I love the sun because you can go to the beach,
The sun is cool and you can get sunburnt.

Gemma Gilmore (12)
Ballee High School

CHRISTMAS EVE NIGHT

Christmas Eve night the snow is falling
Making every object white
It's on the leaves of trees
Falling on everything in sight

All the children are sleeping
Tucked up peacefully in their beds
With all the thoughts of Christmas
Circling around in their heads

They've made their lists and pinned the stockings
Upon the chimney breast
In the hope that they'd be given
All the toys that they like best

Away in the clouds above
Santa Claus and his reindeers fly
They make the journey with the presents
Across the world in the night sky

He'll leave gifts for all the children
To find on Christmas Day
They'll have lots of new exciting games
Which they will be able to play

Gemma Greenwood (12)
Ballee High School

CAPRICORN

My star sign says I'm really cool
But my friends think I'm a bit of a fool.
My star sign says I tend to be shy
But my friends all say that's a definite lie.

My star sign says that when I marry
He's going to be rich and drive a Ferrari.
My star sign says my future looks bright
I really hope my star sign is right.

Laura-Lee Kane (13)
Ballee High School

MID-SUMMER MURDERS

There's a place called Mid-Summer,
Lots of people get killed, some die.
Some people get poisoned, some disappear,
There's a place called Mid-Summer, I lived there.

There's a place called Mid-Summer,
A person got killed there today.
A person will die there tomorrow,
Five have been murdered this week.

There's a place called Mid-Summer,
Not very many people live there.
They're nearly all dead,
I have to go, Heaven is waiting for me.

Jamie McKay (12)
Ballee High School

MY FRIEND

I have a very special friend
I love her very much
She is furry and very soft to touch
And I know she loves me too

She sometimes gets into trouble
Even though she doesn't mean to
It often happens to me
It also happens to you

So now I'll tell what it is
This little friend of mine
It's my dog, my little friend
Who's happy all the time.

Kylie Magill (12)
Ballee High School

MY ZODIAC FAMILY

D   ana lives on the moon,
A   way from her brother,
N   o one knows she's there,
A   nd not even her mother.

C   hloe lives on Mars,
H   ear her sing,
L   ife with the stars, she's
O   ver on the moon,
E   veryone can see her living on Mars.

Dana Curtis (13)
Ballee High School

ZODIAC

He is famous,
He's in big books,
He is in dictionaries and encyclopaedias,
They describe him by using words like
apparent,
paths,
astrology and
the twelve constellations.

Zodiac is my best friend!

Musharat Nara (14)
Ballee High School

THERE IS A MONSTER BELOW MY BED

There is a monster below my bed,
And I've just found out his name is Fred.
The colour of his hair is flaming red,
It shines like a beacon being constantly fed.
My mum thinks I'm mad and shouts 'Get him a doctor,'
But Fred is not something out of Harry Potter.
I know he is watching me all the time,
Sitting there drinking his lemon and lime.
At night he gets up and goes downstairs,
And plays with my pup and eats my chocolate éclairs.
So that was the monster below my bed,
Yep, that's him, my monster Fred.

Samuel Steele (11)
Ballymena Academy

VALENTINE DAY MUDDLE

I met a boy I really liked
Set out to win his heart.
When the time came to say goodnight
I'd always fall apart.
I'd giggle like I had no brain
And then I'd start to cough,
I thought my tomato ketchup stain
Would put the fella off!

My nose would twitch, my legs would shake,
I'd flop into a fever,
On country rambles we would take
Long walks beside the river.
He looked deep into my eyes,
He clutched my hand so gently,
And then he said to my surprise,
'My father has a Bentley!'

Sense came at last and I could see
The future now seemed clear,
He loved the Bentley more than me,
A stupid fool my dear!
So on this most romantic day,
Girls don't set your sights too far.
It's best to turn the other way,
Our rival is the car!

Rachel Hamilton (14)
Ballymena Academy

I HATE SCHOOL

It's a Monday morning,
Another new day,
I put on my coat,
Then I'm on my way.

I stare at the puddles on the ground,
The rain is beating on my head,
Splish, splash, splash goes the rain,
'I hate school,' I said.

Philip Coulter (12)
Ballymena Academy

OUR BEAUTIFUL WORLD

Have you even taken time to look all around you?
Beyond the hustle and bustle of traffic and people,
Away from the clanking of man-made machines,
But into the beauty of our wonderful world.

Have you ever tasted the very air that you breathe?
Beyond the smoke and stink of city fuels,
Out into the country where the fresh grass grows,
Deep in the beauty of our wonderful world.

Have you ever looked closely at the wild growing flowers?
How each tiny petal is so perfectly formed,
Even all the diamonds in the whole earth,
Have not got the wealth and pride of them.

Have you ever watched the birds gathering together?
Getting ready to fly away over the hills,
Have you ever wondered to yourself,
Who told them it was time to go?

Have you ever heard the little grasshoppers,
Making their own beautiful music?
Has it ever made you wonder,
Who taught them to compose?

Alison Beattie (13)
Ballymena Academy

THOSE LOVED ARE ALWAYS HATED

I hate the way it rains,
When the sun wants to shine.
I hate the way when I look,
He doesn't even glance.
I hate the way when my favourite song is on,
He's my favourite thought.
I hate the way when I cry,
He's not there to dry the tears.
I hate the way I want the call
And I'm still waiting.
I hate the way when I dream
And I wake; I notice it was a dream.
I hate the way as time goes by,
Neither the love nor hate die.
But then again, life goes on
And although he never was there and never will be.
There are those who care,
When the dreams turn bad,
When the stars stop spinning.
I'm lying alone in the dark,
Realising that in my heart I don't hate him,
Not a bit,
Not even a little bit,
Not at all.

Sarah Bell (15)
Ballymena Academy

THE ZODIAC

Stars that encircle the Earth?
8 degrees each side of the ecliptic?
All planets inside the belt?
The motion of the celestial sphere?

12 sections, each well known?
Named after constellations?
After Greek, circle of animals?
Connected with all four seasons?

It's all nonsense!

David Manson (13)
Ballymena Academy

A TIGER'S EYE

A tiger's eye is watchful,
It watches day and night
And seeks her prey
By scent, sound and sight

A scent in the air,
A crackle underfoot,
A movement in the shrubs,
A hearty meal for a mother and her cubs

With military precision,
The tiger advances on her prey,
The slightest little movement
And the deer will run away

But hunger is a desperate need,
It drives the tiger on,
A blur . . .
And the deer's brief life is gone

Peter Coulter (13)
Ballymena Academy

A FUSION OF COLOURS

Colours fill our world with happiness and joy,
Blue makes me feel cold,
Like icicles on a frosty winter's morning.
Red makes me feel warm,
Like a fiery hot summer's day.
Yellow makes me feel happy,
Like golden buttercups dancing in the breeze.
Purple makes me think of violence
And anger, which is happening all over our world today.
Pink makes me think of embarrassment,
People making fools of themselves.
Green makes me think of freshly mown grass,
White makes me think of a crisp white shirt,
Ready for your first day at school.
Black makes me think of darkness,
Like stepping into the unknown.
But the colour that I like the best
Is the golden glow of the early morning sunrise.

Grace McBurney (14)
Ballymena Academy

LITTLE SISTERS

My sisters are so annoying,
they scream and cry all day,
they only care about themselves
and are always the centre of attention.

They fight and shout all the time,
just to cause havoc,
but if you ignore them, they shout even louder
and they're a pack of mischief makers.

If they're sent to bed, they start to cry,
unless you tell a story,
and if they don't like it, you'd better cover your ears,
but they always get their way.

After a hard day's screaming,
they're always very tired,
this is when I love them the most,
when their eyes are shut and their mouths are closed.

David McCooke (13)
Ballymena Academy

WOULDN'T IT BE GREAT

Cast away on a desert island
Wouldn't it be great.
The sun would shine, the sea would sparkle,
But I'd be lost without a mate.

No school and no more homework
Wouldn't that be great.
But without holidays to look forward to
What would I celebrate?

So much time to relax and unwind
Wouldn't it be great.
I'd have to be careful to mark each day
Or I'd lose track of the date.

My shiny bubble has been burst,
Paradise now seems cursed.
Yet I want my dream to return,
To feel the sea, the sand and the sun.
Everything to seem first rate,
Now wouldn't that be great.

Claire Ferguson (14)
Ballymena Academy

THE ZODIAC

Reading your horoscope is quite common now,
While years ago people would not know how.
Your birthday indicates what star sign you are,
Which originates from space a long way afar.

Our outlook is predicted by the moon, planets and sun,
Astrologers must find their job really fun.
Powerful telescopes can detect the motions of the sky,
Which all take place away up high.

The history of astrology goes back a long way,
And it looks like it is here to stay.
From ancient Babylonia it spread to here,
But many thought it was false and slightly queer.

The first horoscope in 409BC was recorded,
The Greeks who thought of this were finally awarded,
The popularity of this since then is steadily rising,
So astrologers can keep their job of advising.

If this propaganda is to be believed or not,
People get enjoyment from the whole lot.
Sometimes I look what Libra has in store
And end up wanting to find out more.

Cheryl Gaston (14)
Ballymena Academy

MY HOME ZOO

A squirrel, two rabbits and an elephant too,
Two cats, two dogs and a kangaroo,
A goldfish called George,
A turtle called Sue,
And a massive talking Winnie The Pooh.

A hamster, a mouse and a guinea pig too,
A fat, mucky hippo called Baloo,
A lion that roars,
A cow that goes moo,
And that is my big, dream home zoo!

Amanda Milligan (13)
Ballymena Academy

HALLOWE'EN NIGHT

What really happens during Hallowe'en night?
Do vampire bats come out to bite?
Do ghosts come out and creep about?
Is that what really happens when the lights go out?

What really happens during Hallowe'en night?
Do witches sit on their brooms and take flight?
Do werewolves stand and bay at the moon?
Is that what really happens when the fireworks go boom?

What really happens during Hallowe'en night?
Do ghouls come out to give people a fright?
Does Dracula awake from the dead?
Is that what really happens when I am snuggled up in bed?

What really happens during Hallowe'en night?
Do the skeletons raise from their burial site?
Is what people say about Hallowe'en right?
Is that what *really* happens during Hallowe'en night?

Laura Sherrey (13)
Ballymena Academy

THE TEDDY BEARS ON TOP OF MY WARDROBE

The teddy bears on top of my wardrobe,
Just sit there, day by day,
Looking in the same direction,
They never get to play.

Poor teddies,
It must be really boring,
But then what do they get up to
Whenever I am snoring?

They probably have a party,
With lots of cakes and sweets,
Not forgetting chocolate bars
And other kinds of treats.

But when the party's over,
The time they probably take,
To clear up all the mess they made,
Before morning, when I wake.

Kathryn Shaw (14)
Ballymena Academy

THE GAME

Rugby is a hooligans' game played by gentlemen,
Football is a gentleman's game played by hooligans,
Although cricket is just a gentleman's game.

Tennis is a game loved around the world,
Squash is a game for the fittest competitors,
Ping-pong is a game for the quickest hand.

Horse riding is the sport of kings,
Athletics is the game of testing your ability,
Gymnastics is the game for the most flexible athletes.

Basketball is a game of accuracy,
Baseball is a game for excellent batting skills,
All sports are just games after all.

Jason Dalrymple (13)
Ballymena Academy

MY FRIEND

My friend was a true friend indeed,
He knew what to do when I was in need,
He would always listen when I had something to say,
And make me laugh day by day.

My friend's advice is always right,
He would sit and chat well into the night,
He would make me happy when I was sad,
And shout at me when I was bad.

My friend was accused of something,
That caused him to be sent away one morning,
Something must have made him angry that day,
Because my friend would never have acted that way.

My friend is gone and I miss him a lot,
But everyone has mostly forgot,
How good a dog he truly was,
And all the laughter that he caused.

Angela Telford (13)
Ballymena Academy

DO YOU KNOW WHAT YOU'RE REALLY LIKE?

Like the crashing waves of the sea, Neptune rules this sign,
King of all waters, he influences the colours of the sea
                                upon every Piscean.
From the deepest blues of the ocean, to the sparkling slivers
                                    on the surface,
A Piscean is mired by vast mood swings.
Though the imagination can run away, so can they,
With escaping a situation coming as second nature.

Buried in the sand, Cancerians prefer peace and harmony.
When they feel threatened, they build a protective shell,
And like a crab, they can only hide away for so long.
They feel truly at peace, while looking at,
The hazy grey above the ocean, and pale blue of the morning sky.

Like the flitter of a fish as it skims through the sea,
Aquarians are different and unpredictable, and forever changing
                                    their minds.
As the fish darts through the glistening waters,
It captures the wondrous colours of pale yellow and green,
The colours, which bring peace and harmony to Aquarians.

With those resilient horns, a ram may be hard to pass,
And alike, an Arian is ready to pummel down any hindrance.
To them the world is a contest; any challenge large or small.
Like a wild ram, they do not like to be fenced in.
As the sun sets an Arian can see the glowing colours of red and gold,
And feel satisfaction for what they have achieved.

The fiery lion stops by the water's side to admire his mane,
Though full of pride and style, he is overpowered by vanity.
With much ambition, Leos act their thoughts in a big way,
Like the mighty roar of the leader of the pack.
Though with the fierce exterior, Leos often need love in their lives,
And may sometimes be too afraid of themselves to ask for it.

Charlotte Knowles (14)
Ballymena Academy

THE ZODIAC

The zodiac's the neighbourhood of the stars,
Turn right at Venus, then left at Mars,
I wish I could fly up there some day,
Have a chat with the galaxy, what would I say?

Take a walk with Leo,
Along Orion's belt,
I heard it's lovely in the summer,
The sun's so hot that I would melt!

I'd have a water fight with the water-carrier,
Fly higher than a British Harrier,
I'd have no worries,
I'd have no cares,
The sky would light up,
Like the brightest of flares.

If only I could
Fly up through the stars,
Turn right at Venus and left at Mars.

James Erwin (12)
Ballymena Academy

THE 'PERFECT' ANSWER

O constellations
How 'fitting' they seem to be
That our life is planned for us
From start to finish.
We need not worry what lies ahead
Because it is all planned.
Well let me tell you something
Many men have wasted their lives
In coming up with these myths
That seem to be the 'perfect' answer
To our modern, busy life.
These signs that appeared to be there from the start
That seem to be able to tell the future
Well let me say this
In the vastness of the universe
And with the laws of probability
There is every chance
That a random position of a few stars
Can mean anything to our tiny deluded minds.
But let me ask this question
These 'answers' tell us what this life holds for us
But what is in store for us when this life
Is no more?

Richard Gilmore (13)
Ballymena Academy

SOMEONE SPECIAL

There is a very special person,
She's kind, generous and very gentle,
If she wasn't here I'm sure I'd go mental!
Whenever I need her, she's always around,
To make sure my feet stay firmly on the ground.

There is a very special person,
When my sister and I have a fight,
She's always there to put things right.
If I call, she'll always come,
It is my very loving mum!

Sarah Pedlow (13)
Ballymena Academy

STARS

What's in the stars today?
What's going to happen today?
Will there be luck?
Will there be adventure?

I've read what's in the stars today,
Yes, there'll be luck,
Yes, there'll be adventure,
Even a spot of romance.

I don't want to know what's going to happen,
Really I don't care,
Your life is meant to be lived,
Lived in wonder of what's going to happen.

Live life to the full is what I've always said,
Don't let pieces of paper rule your life,
You don't need someone to tell you what will happen,
You need to decide that for yourself.

Live each day as a new day,
You only have one life so live it,
And don't let silly star signs
Live it for you.

Heather Darby (12)
Ballymena Academy

THE ZODIAC

The zodiac, what's that, a joke?
Whoever made it up must have been a right old bloke.
When I heard it at first I thought it was a horse,
Or tale of a geezer by the name of Norse.

The bit that confuses me most
Is that it's written in everything, even the past.
And is it true what they say?
It tells everything that happens in your boring old day?

By the way, what have animals got to do with stars?
And why are they named after scales and
Fishermen who wish to have really fast cars?

I don't believe it, not one bit,
And when people mention it I just burst into a fit.
Because if it was really true,
The believers in numbers would be more than a few.

Who has ever heard of Capricorn or Leo?
And with Gemini, that makes a pretty strange trio.
I don't like the way people go on,
Talking gibberish at the crack of dawn.

None of my mates believe it and neither do I,
Now come on, you don't either - don't deny.
I know there's only one true God, that I believe,
But you can believe your daily newspaper
Which you're going to retrieve.

There's one last thing I have to say,
It's a pile of rubbish and that's my way.
If you believe it, you've gone off your head,
But go on and believe it from morning till bed.

Timothy Bamber (13)
Ballymena Academy

THE SECRET WORLD

As I walked down the road,
On a dark, lonely night,
A man jumped round the corner,
And gave me quite a fright.

When he ran on past,
I thought all was well,
I continued to walk,
And suddenly I fell.

Down, down, down,
Through a hole in the ground,
My life flashed before me
Then I landed and listened to the sound.

Whispering, mumbling, chatting away,
I looked up and couldn't believe my eyes,
Lots of people staring at me,
I was as surprised to see them, as they were to see me.

It was magical,
A fairy tale, underground habitat,
They picked me up and turned me around,
And we started to chat.

'This is our little secret,
We hope you won't tell,
To us this heaven,
To you it is hell.'

They sent me back up,
In a puff of smoke,
And to this day,
My promise is not broke.

Louise Stirling (13)
Ballymena Academy

THE ZODIAC

The zodiac are stars placed in the sky
An ancient tradition passed on from generation to generation
Believed by the Greeks in an extinct civilisation
But somehow still carries the same meaning

>The Aztecs and Greeks believed the same thing
>That this really was a miraculous thing
>The stars in the sky burning bright in the darkness
>Burning like lanterns, illuminating the sky

People have long trusted the stars
Their amazing mystical powers
But people have changed
Beliefs have evolved
Time to move on
Without our beautiful stars.

Ben Kennedy (13)
Ballymena Academy

SCORPIO - 23RD OCTOBER - 22ND NOVEMBER

Scorpio, 8th sign of the zodiac
Serious scorpions in all they do
Would rather be killed than kill
A hard working breed
A fact no one can deny them
A group ruled by Mars, the god of war, a warrior
Easily raised, bad temper is feared
Very, very powerful
Competitiveness renowned
Will never quit where fear is found
Scorpio, my sign
The best of them all.

Alan Norton (12)
Ballymena Academy

My Zodiac

Pisces:

Saturn turns your mind to finding a secure base for your life,
As far as I'm concerned I'm happy in my own home,
Love will come near when you meet your mates for a drink,
Well, I'm afraid I'm under 21 and they wouldn't serve me
so that's that done with,
Put a higher value on your job skills and others will too,
Well, I'm still at school and I don't have a job,
so scrap that one too,
Luck sings with five pals,
I don't have a singing voice so I'll not be singing,

My day has gone nothing like my zodiac,
but perhaps it might someday.

Andrew Robinson (13)
Ballymena Academy

Zodiac

I was born under the sign of Capricorn
Mum says it suits me because I'm a silly goat
But I think astrology is nonsense
We are all individuals, not just twelve
different types,
I don't believe in luck or fate or 'the stars' -
We need to make our own luck
By doing our best and being determined to succeed.
No matter what my stars say is in store for me
I'm going to make today and every day a good day
just by being me.

Stephen Donaldson (12)
Ballymena Academy

ZODIAC

There is a place up in the clouds
Where we are not allowed -

There's Pisces and Aquarius
The water signs
Nothing can tear them apart
Not even a merman!

Then there are Aries and Virgo
The glamour girls
They spend all their time at the mall
Laughing and giggling like long-lost sisters.

Of course then there is Leo and Scorpio
The tough girls
They love to play tag team wrestling
It's their favourite activity.

There's Cancer and Capricorn
The reality girls
Everyone turns to them
When they have a problem.

Last but not least
Gemini, Libra, Sagittarius and Taurus
They are so close
Yet so different.

All these girls live up in the clouds
Predicting our future
In their own world
In luxury.

They are with you forever
All best friends
Your own special zodiac
Forever.

Catherine Lynn (13)
Ballymena Academy

IT'S ALL IN THE STARS

A bucket of water splashed onto the maiden,
'It wasn't my fault' said the water carrier.
'The crab nipped me and my bucket fell.'
'It wasn't my fault,' said the crab,
'The archer scared me and I jumped.'
'It wasn't my fault,' said the archer,
'The bull was chasing me and I tried to shoot it
            with my arrow.'
'It wasn't my fault,' said the bull,
'The lion was trying to attack me.'
'It wasn't my fault,' said the lion,
'I stepped on the fish and slid.'
'It wasn't my fault,' said the fish,
'I fell off the scales.'
'It wasn't our fault,' said the scales,
'The goat put her foot on us and made us unbalanced.'
'It wasn't my fault,' said the goat,
'The ram headbutted me.'
'It wasn't my fault,' said the ram,
'The scorpion stung me.'
'It wasn't my fault,' said the scorpion,
'The twins were teasing me.'
'It wasn't our fault,' said the twins,
'It's all in the stars.'

Lynne McCosh (12)
Ballymena Academy

ZODIAC

There are twelve signs in the zodiac,
Twelve constellations in the sky.
Each made up of stars,
Each with an animal, name and sign.

Aries, the ram; the quick thinker and doer,
And a very enthusiastic person you are.

Taurus, the bull; persistent, reliable,
But you tend to be stubborn.

Gemini, the twins; always on your toes,
Chatty, sociable and highly imaginative.

Cancer, the crab; curious, complex,
And you can be very emotional.

Leo, the lion; proud, ambitious,
And always wanting to be the centre of attention.

Virgo, the virgin; cautious, self-reliant,
And you are such a perfectionist.

Libra, the scales; co-operative, self-expressing,
You have a powerful sense of fair play.

Scorpio, the scorpion; strong, wilful,
You like to be in control.

Sagittarius, the archer; honest, straightforward,
And you create excitement wherever you go.

Capricorn, the goat; patient, realistic, responsible,
And you can be easily embarrassed.

Aquarius, the water carrier; honest, sincere,
You love to be different.

Pisces, the fish; sensitive, lack willpower,
Susceptible to the thoughts and feelings of others.

These are the signs of the zodiac,
Does yours describe you?

Joel Hutchinson (13)
Ballymena Academy

THE ZODIAC

I am a maiden fair and true,
This star sign will look after you,
And at the end, if you should wait,
Then you shall also find your fate.

For at the start when you are born,
You get a star sign, maybe Capricorn,
Libra, Aries, Pisces too,
But I am a maiden fair and true.

I am a star sign, not a ram,
Can you guess which one I am?
I am not a fish or a lion,
I'll tell you again, I am a maiden.

My hair is brown, blonde or black,
My skin is so soft too,
My face is round and nicely shaped,
My eyes are green, brown or blue.

That's right, I'm a Virgo,
The best star sign too, I am a maiden,
Fair and true.

Alex Loxley (13)
Ballymena Academy

ZODIAC

Darkness has fallen, the stars are shining bright,
Zodiac comes alive in the depth of the night.
What sign are you, could you be like me?
For I am the ram, I am an Aries.

Are you the lion which is the Leo,
Or could you be the fierce Scorpio.
Look up at the stars to see,
For I am the ram, I am an Aries.

Some people believe, some people think it's rubbish,
Pisces are level-headed, they are the fish.
Gaze up at the beautiful night sky,
For that it where the secret of zodiac lies.

Alison Young (12)
Ballymena Academy

TAURUS

If you are a Taurean
Your astrology sign is a bull
The horns of a bull
The temper of a bull
But this short-tempered animal
Has a nice side to him
You are conservative
You are practical and possessive
You can be strong-willed
And also obstinate

Taureans are born between
April and May
Your element is earth
Your planet is Venus
Your stone is emerald
Your metal is copper
And best of all you will
Share your sign with *me!*

Mark Kerr (12)
Ballymena Academy

CIRCLE OF LIFE

If the circle of life was a zoo,
What would you go to see?
Would you go to see the colourful flowers
Or the sweet smelling jacaranda tree?
Would you go to see the snakes slithering slowly across the ground,
Or hear the lion's powerful roar?
Would you go to see the latest product of civilisation,
A CCTV society at work?
In the curious world in which we live,
We are no longer able to walk the streets in anonymity.
Almost everywhere we go a camera follows us.
I do not know what I would go to see,
There are so many things.
What would you go to see?

Emma Boyd (14)
Ballymena Academy

THE ZODIAC ATTACK

I know for a fact they are coming,
A punishment for non-believers.

First the raging bull will come charging in,
Wrecking all who try to stop him,
Then will come the archer great,
Breaking up date by date,
The scales in all their shining glory,
Will make this fight look a lot less gory,
The water carrier will then appear,
Her foul-tasting water is something to fear,
The twins will then be seen not heard,
Confusing all who have ever been,
To see the fish in the big blue stream.

The roaring lion he will then come,
Scaring all who are very young,
The scorpion with its stinger great,
Will attack everybody but he will be late,
The ram and the goat will have been and gone,
And will have left everybody with a violent pong,
The crab in all his splendour and might,
Will make sure the zodiac signs win this fight,
The maiden will act like a damsel in distress,
When anyone comes near she will make them confess,
To the awful crimes that she will suggest.

I know for a fact they are coming,
Maybe the stars will tell us when.

Steven Carson (12)
Ballymena Academy

Zodiac

I looked up at the sky last night,
and saw a bunch of stars so bright.
They started racing up and down the sky,
enjoying the cool breeze as morning was nigh.

The next night I went there was a change,
they looked like a different range.
I think they were Aquarius,
but they all really looked the same to us.

The stars were shining brightly now,
I think they must be having a row.
Some of them are bossy and are starting to rule,
and now are forming a very large bull.

Some are jumping and flying around,
you'd think they were nearly touching the ground.
Their gold colour and bright shine,
some look as if they are really kind.

Every night I go out,
there is always a smiling star about.
Even if the rain falls down,
a bit misty, but not one with a frown.

Out of all the zodiac gang,
there is a favourite one of mine.
This is a small and bright little group,
which turned out to be a brave, strong troop.

Rachael Laughlin (12)
Ballymena Academy

ZODIAC

Dark nights, starry skies,
Do you believe the stories,
About what's just before our eyes?
The signs of the zodiac,
Are they true?
Or are they just silly ideas to you?
How do we know,
What is the truth?
If the zodiac signs are true,
What do they say about you?
Are you the bull, the crab,
The ram or the goat?
Is twenty your lucky number,
Forty or thirty-two?
Is your lucky day
Monday, Wednesday or Sunday?
Are you really intelligent, lucky,
Witty and thoughtful?
Is your lucky colour
Pink, orange or blue?
How will you feel this week?
Excited, depressed or cross?
Can these things really tell you
What will happen in your life?
Or are they just a lot of nonsense,
Made up by old wives?
This decision as to what to believe
Is now left up to you.
Are these things made up,
Or are they really true?

Lyndsey Hamill (13)
Ballymena Academy

BARRIERS

She sat
Looking out of the window
Watching the rain
Trickle down the steaming pane.
A reflection
A cloudy mirror of her tears,
Running down her face
She would be all right,
The sun was soon to appear
Her tears soon to dry.
Or would they?

She sat
Looking out of the window
Listening to the wind
Its endless moaning
Its presumptuous restlessness
Suddenly to cease
As if for breath.
Then launching into its mindless howling
This was her, deep inside
Screaming to get out.
Yelling for help
Someone soon to hear her,
Someone was sure to unlock that door.
The steadfast wall,
Unyielding to no one,
That locked her in
And everyone out.
Someone was soon to save her
Or would they?

Stephanie McKervill (14)
Ballymena Academy

STAR CONVERSATION

Sagittarius, the archer, looks up to the sky,
But instead of more stars, a splash of water meets his eye.
Empty is the bucket of the water bearer, Aquarius,
'You made me all wet!' argues the archer, Sagittarius.
'It was not my fault' says Aquarius, alarmed,
'The bull, Taurus, nudged me, he has horns, he was armed!'
Taurus, overhearing, plodded over to intervene,
'It was the crab's fault - he nipped me with his pincers,
he was far too keen!'
Said Cancer the crab, 'Blame Gemini the twins, they chased me
here and there.'
Together Gemini cried, 'The goat told us it was a dare.'
'Leo the lion said he'd eat me if I didn't,' said Capricorn the goat.
'The maiden Virgo said she wouldn't feed me, so I thought
I'd better get something down my throat!'
Virgo said 'I had to save Pisces the fish, for they were out of water!'
Pisces chimed in 'Aries tossed us out because he's a bad tempered
old rotter!'
Aries began to yell and shout, 'It's Libra, it's her - I was getting
myself weighed when she flung me into the pond and wet my fur!'
The scales chorused 'I was hit with an arrow from a bow -
Sagittarius flung his too low!'
'It wasn't my fault' cried Sagittarius,
'It was him, over there. It was Aquarius!'

Suzanne Smyth (13)
Ballymena Academy

STAR SIGNS

Some people live by them,
Their lives totally engulfed by them,
Star signs.

First thing every morning,
When the daily newspaper arrives,
Star signs.

What about the television,
On the daily programmes,
Star signs.

There is always the phone line,
Dial a number to get your,
Star signs.

They are on the internet,
On special sites,
Star signs.

We could have our own astrologer,
Giving us our,
Star signs.

Many people don't make a decision,
Without consulting their,
Star signs.

John Carson (12)
Ballymena Academy

A SCORPIO STAR SIGN

I have a Scorpio star sign,
I read it in the paper.
It said that I was to have a wonderful day,
but guess what happened later.
It was a Saturday,
I was to bale some hay,
but when it was on the trailer,
it fell off and made me flatter.
I had to pile it on again,
but this time it went aflame,
I put it out with water,
which made the hay softer.
I told my dad,
which made him look sad.
I ran back home,
to go to a phone,
but I got lost on the way.
Oh, what a day.
Now I'm in hospital,
because I got lost a little.

Alan Scroggie (12)
Ballymena Academy

IN SEARCH OF THE MEANING OF LIFE

I went in search of the meaning of life,
One day while I was at school.
I asked my science teacher,
So he chucked me in the (biology) pool.

I asked my PE teacher,
So he made me run a mile,
After that he told me
To go ask Mrs Lyle.

Mrs Lyle was busy,
So I asked Mr McQueen,
But he was rather mean.

After this I went to see,
A mystic man called Tool,
He pointed at the stars,
And I said, 'Don't be such a fool!'

Andrew Scott (13)
Ballymena Academy

THE ZODIAC

Think of all the stars in the sky,
Twinkling, glittering, smiling.
Troubled lives in a mysterious world of their own,
Looking down on this troublesome world.

Too many stars, too many to count,
Each forming patterns of their own.
As we gently sleep in our cosy beds,
Thunder roars as constellations are formed.

Hiding as murderous clouds pass them by,
Peeping through the still darkness,
Dancing in the bright moonlight,
Then disappearing at the break of the morn.

Leo, Scorpio, Virgo and Capricorn,
Each with their own magical meanings.
Shouting out loud and staring into space,
We wonder as they give us no clues to their secret lives.

Laura McKelvey (13)
Ballymena Academy

JENNY SURGENOR

Jenny is a 'tooti-fruiti' kind of girl
A 'Do you want a sweet?'
Kind of girl

A
> Pizza and chips
> Sandwiches
> Milkybar

Kind of friend

She is a
> Very arty
> Let's go to a party
> Having fun
> Let's play in the sun
> Want to have a chat?

Kind of girl

A
> Boy crazy
> Never lazy
> Giggly
> Wiggly

Kind of friend

She collects
> Funny jokes
> Sweetie wrappers
> Toy cats

And is a champion
> Smiler
> Perfectionist with hair
> Laughter
> Friend

And is someone
Who
Would give anyone
Her last Rolo
Kind of friend.

Rachel Rainey (12)
Ballymena Academy

A PLAYFUL NIGHT

Leo the lion bright in the sky
Playing with Taurus as fat as a pie
Cappy the Capricorn wants to play too
Now the night sky is turning into a zoo

Virgo is playing snooker as usual
Cancer and Libra are in a bamboozle!
Gemini is trying to get in on the fun
While Scorpio is eating a great big bun!

Sagittarius and Pisces are having a row
No one is going near them right now
Aquarius is watching over it all
Hoping it won't turn into a brawl

Aquarius is trying to break up a fight
While Aries is going round in great flight
Aries has landed, Aquarius has won
Leo and Taurus have finished their fun

All is peaceful as it should be
The sun is up, it's time for tea
And time for the star signs to go to bed
They all think it's time to rest their heads.

David McCrory (12)
Ballymena Academy

GILLIAN GILLESPIE

My best friend is a fast kind of friend
A 'do you want a race?'
Kind of friend

A
    Salad
    Chicken
    Doughnut
    Belgian waffle
    Mints
Kind of friend

She is a
    Clean my bedroom
    Go to the shops
    Do my hair
    Get my homework done
    Let's have fun
Kind of girl

A
    'Hello boys!'
    Always
    Near
    'Never fear'
Kind of friend

She collects
    Dog stickers
    Ornaments
    Books
    She calls everyone by a funny name
    And was a champion

Laughter
Joker
Eater
Shopper
And mint sucker
She is someone
Who
Would always
Make you laugh.

Ashley Craig (11)
Ballymena Academy

FASHION FOR THE STARS

Bright and happy,
Yellow, green or blue,
These are the only colours Aries will do.
While traditional colours like grey and green,
Are the only colours of Capricorn I mean.
Taurus will only be seen in green,
Aquarius wear what they like,
As long as it's bright.
Cancer like it smart and classy,
Pisces like it very sassy.
Leo like it warm and sunny,
Gemini like value for money.
While Virgos are bargain hunters,
And Libra like it subtle.
Unlike Scorpio's sleek and sexy numbers,
Sagittarius will always be top,
On them you will never need to call a fashion cop!

Lauren Houston (12)
Ballymena Academy

MY FRIEND

My friend is a chocolate lover kind of friend
'Do you want some sweets?' kind of friend

A
>Milkybar Chunky
>Dairy Milk
>Fruit and nut bar
>Chocolate Buttons
>Wispa bar

Kind of friend

He is a
>Smart
>Good on a flight simulator
>Slow moving
>Good at maths
>Food fisher

Kind of friend

A
>Shy
>Nervy
>Husky
>Slow at work
>Never brushes his teeth

Kind of friend

He collects
>Dead bodies
>Frogs
>Newts
>Flight simulator
>PlayStations

Kind of friend

He is a champion at
              Picking a fight with someone
              Working the computer
              Taking things slowly
              Wearing a jumper all the time
              Eating chocolate
Kind of friend

He would give you his last Rolo if he liked you
Kind of friend.

Ryan Walker (12)
Ballymena Academy

THE ZODIAC

As I gaze at the sky at night
I am amazed at the amount of light
Countless stars, bright flashing lights
Though if you look closer
You will soon find out
There are twelve constellations about
Capricorn, Aquarius, Pisces, Sagittarius
Taurus, Gemini, Cancer, Aries
Leo, Virgo and Libra and last but not least Scorpio
Each have their own date and sign
With that comes along a meaning
Which one are you?
Even mine does not suit me
So from now on when I look up at the night sky
I just appreciate the amazing beauty
But for me to believe in all the meanings
Sounds a little crazy.

Richard Ross (12)
Ballymena Academy

Amy Colgan

Amy is an always laughing, comical, kind of friend
A 'Do you want to talk about it?'
Kind of friend.

A
    Chicken sandwich
    with lots of salt
    and a yoghurt
    for dessert
Kind of girl.

She is a
    'Are you busy
    want to talk?'
    Piano playing
    Having fun
Kind of girl.

A
    'Don't worry
    Christine.
    I believe you!'
Kind of girl

She collects
    Posters of her
    favourite band
    and lovely
    smelling pens

And was a champion
        Runner
        Trampolinist
        And friend.

She's the sort of person
who'd get a laugh out of
a wet hen.

Christine McBurney (12)
Ballymena Academy

STARGAZER

Far up high
In that black ocean sky
The stars are twinkling
I lay and gaze up at them
And they are secretly winking
To me back down on Earth

So many planets
Whizzing and whirring around
But they are all gravity bound

The only place
In open space
There is a world with no gravity
This is the black hole!

What is in the black hole
We don't have a clue
I suspect you would be thrown
Into the unknown.

Victoria Murdock (12)
Ballymena Academy

KATIE NIKLAS

Katie was a tomato kind of friend
'Do you want some juice with your breakfast?'
Kind of friend.

A
       spiced chicken
       white bread
       pancakes
Kind of girl

She was a
       dancer for everyone
       she jumped, skipped
       and hopped
       tapped and twirled
       curtsied and bowed
Kind of girl

A
       'Hi Inès!'
       fun and laughter
       bouncy, happy
       'That's a sin!'
Kind of friend

She collected
              Medals . . . by the tonne!
              Old fashioned stories
              Bandannas
              Photographs and drawings

She was a
          soft
          gentle
          playful
          funny
          and not greedy
Kind of a person.

She was someone who
shared everything
with me.

Inès Delpy (11)
Ballymena Academy

SONNET ON PLANETS
SEPTEMBER 2001

Some say man's fate is written in the stars;
That understanding of the constellations
Can guide his way; that Jupiter or Mars
May seal man's doom by their configurations.
Was it the sun in Virgo that gave rise
To acts of terror by the Taliban?
Positions of the stars in evening skies
That shouted vengeance on Afghanistan?
Must world events, the future of a nation,
Or human fortune, length of time on Earth
Be quantified and settled in relation
To planets, at the moment of man's birth?
No! A wise being from a higher sphere
Governs all things, and hovers very near.

Rebecca Knowles (12)
Ballymena Academy

Carla Robinson

My best friend is a great kind of friend
A 'Let's go have some fun.'
Kind of friend.

A
    Go down town
    brown bread
    vibrant colours
    reading books
Kind of friend.

She is a
    Make people happy
    play hockey
    great fun
    always happy
Kind of friend.

A
    'Hi there!'
    always there
    'Oh dear!'
    'Don't fear!'
Kind of friend.

She collects
    Good books
    funny things
    and other bits and pieces.

She is a champion
> Friend
> eater
> sleeper
> and scary movie lover

She is someone
who
could never get
down in the dumps.

Rachel Heaney (12)
Ballymena Academy

DREAMS

Before I go to bed at night
I always turn off the light,
Then I creep into my bed
And gently lay down my head,
Suddenly I drift into a dream,
What do I see? A mountain of ice cream.
I've dreamt for years and it's finally come true,
Help me someone what should I do?
I shout but there's no one there,
It must be that nobody cares,
I don't care I've got my wish,
Not it's time to empty this dish,
My bedroom door opens with a *boom,*
There's my mum in my room,
I look up and there she stands,
'Why are you licking your hands?'
I told her I was eating ice cream,
'Go back to bed, it's only a dream.'

Steven Kernoham (14)
Ballymena Academy

The Zodiac

In the sky at night you see
Constellations one, two, three.
Aries is the sign of action,
Taurus is the gourmet type
Whilst Gemini is the smartest one.
Cancer is a friend that's ripe,
The ambitious lion, Leo by name
Can't beat Virgo who thinks disorder's lame.
Libra's the judge in the court of zodiac,
Scorpio is the destructive and psychic attack.
Sagittarius the adventurist, is all for the task,
When Capricorn the courageous is willing to ask.
Aquarius the rebel and Pisces the fish
Are last but not least on the zodiac dish.

Neil Paul
Ballymena Academy

Nature

The beauty of nature
Has yet to be discovered,
The trees, the birds, the flowers,
The trees swaying gently
The birds chirping with glee.
As they bath in the puddles
Warmed by the sunshine.
The tree blossoms in spring
The snow in winter,
All Mother Nature's way
Of showing the world's beauty
To its full potential.

Nicole McBurney (13)
Ballymena Academy

CIRCLE OF LIFE

Capricorn, the organised pessimist,
Aquarius, restless, passionate and free,
Loveable Pisces cries for my soul.
Mind and body infuse to make Aries,
Stubborn Taurus sits and rests
Whilst youthful Gemini busies around.
Cancer, quiet, has an awful sharp tongue,
Ongoing Leo shows off to the rest.
Demanding Virgo discriminates and fusses
As diplomatic Libra fairly judges a case.
Mystical Scorpio's magnetic energy
Attracts honest Sagittarius like a flake of steel.
These zodiac signs, we can't comprehend,
Remain a mystery of the black night sky.

Roddy Montgomery (12)
Ballymena Academy

THE ZODIAC

The star sign is fishes,
The 12th and final sign of the zodiac,
Pisceans are psychic and sensitive,
Lovable but are hurt easily,
Dates from 18th February to 19th March,
Watch out, watch out,
The Pisceans are about!

Adam Brady (12)
Ballymena Academy

THE ZODIAC

I sit alone on the bench,
For I am a lonely child.
I stare into the dark sky,
And dream of fantasies wild.

As I look into the night sky,
Tears glisten in my eyes.
For up above I see a shape,
Which makes me want to cry.

A friendly goat peers down at me,
And smiles a thoughtful smile.
He whispers some soothing words,
To make my heart go wild.

A friend at last I have gained,
A whoop of joy I throw.
My loneliness is gone,
But now a name I need to know.

'My name is Capricorn,' he replied,
'Emily' I told him too.
We chatted for hours upon end,
About the past, the present and the future new.

But soon our time came to an end,
And our departure drew near.
A friend I have gained and a friend I have lost,
But once again I brush away that lonely tear.

Jenny Marshall (12)
Ballymena Academy

AUTUMN FUN!

The autumn time is coming,
The winds are getting strong,
All the leaves are falling,
And nights are getting long.

The leaves are changing colour,
The trees are getting bare,
Summer flowers are dying,
And bright colours now are rare.

Some birds are heading south,
For warmer lands to go,
Some creatures gather seeds and nuts
Before the winter snow.

Now Hallowe'en approaches
With promises of fright,
And people now are wary
Of everything in sight.

The children with their sparklers
Watch fireworks galore,
Bangers, rockets, fountains
And many, many more.

Then when it all is over,
And all is said and done,
You really do have to admit
Autumn has been fun!

Paul Lamont (12)
Ballymena Academy

THE PILOT

The jet taxis down to the end of the runway,
The pilot then waits for the take-off signal from the control tower
and makes a final pre-flight check.
Then the jet is hurled down the runway at a rate of knots.
The jet finally leaves the runway and the landing gear is lifted up
from beneath it like three mechanical legs.
Now it's thirty minutes cruising over the vast desert waste to the target,
when the pilot reaches the bomb run he brings up his array of weapons.
He then designates the target, his finger hovers menacingly over the
weapon-release switch.
He prepares to launch his missile and travelling at ten miles a minute
there's no room for error.
He launches his raging bull and it hits the target like the fist of God,
For the surrounding onlookers on the ground, it was like a colossal
hammer had hit the ground.
For the pilot however, it was just another mission.

Andrew Shields (14)
Ballymena Academy

HEADACHE

When I woke up this morning,
And then got out of my bed,
I felt little people banging
With hammers inside of my head.

I finally dragged myself to school
And told my friend of my trouble.
She nagged and nagged at me
To go to sick bay on the double.

The white walls and the skylight,
Went straight to my head,
All that I really wanted
Was to be tucked up in my own bed.

The teacher finally phoned my mum
She came and got me at three,
I'm in my little bed now
And the headache's now gone. *Yippee!*

Kirsty Robinson (14)
Ballymena Academy

DANCING

Think of all those animals and
People from the stars.
Dancing around the world together.
Do you ever wonder what they're
Dancing to? They're dancing to the
Sound of the stars twinkling.

It all began when Sagittarius
(The leader) was listening to the stars
Twinkling and he started to dance
And the rest followed and they became
Trapped forever dancing around the world.
Only changing when the planets move.

So next time you read your
Star sign, think of the people and animals
Of the stars, forever trapped.
Forever dancing.

Judy McAllister (12)
Ballymena Academy

AUTUMN

Autumn is here once again,
The same old traditions are just the same,
The fireworks going *boom, boom, boom!*
With Hallowe'en releasing *gloom, gloom, gloom!*

Autumn is here once again,
The leaves are falling just the same,
All different colours of leaves,
Falling from above, from the trees.

Autumn is here once again,
The temperature drops just the same,
Puddles of rain are frozen,
The harsh cold winds are blowing.

Autumn is here once again,
The fruit is ripening just the same,
Apples turn red waiting to be picked,
Raspberries there to be licked.

Autumn is here once again,
Autumn is here just the same.

David Frew (13)
Ballymena Academy

SPACE

A pitch-black darkness which may go on forever
With stars, sun, planets and moon,
Will we ever find an end to space?
If we do, it won't happen any time soon.

Is there intelligent life out there
Or are we all alone in space?
A never-ending darkness, all to ourselves,
Could humans be the only intelligent race?

It will take us forever to see all of space,
Many places we will never find,
But we'll never stop searching, even if we know
That the search will never end.

Jonathan Jackson (13)
Ballymena Academy

DO YOU BELIEVE?

Never have I seen a sight
as beautiful as the starry night.
To watch it glitter all the time
around me, it stops time.

To think every little star
Each away, so very far.
Can they tell us what to do
to carry on or start anew?

Do they tell us what we're going to be
happy, sad or with family?
Are we stubborn or are we giving
will we make what's worth of living?

For when we are all gone
the stars shall still sing their song.
A song of beauty, wisdom too,
the tale of what was me and you.

So do you believe in the zodiac sign
that it will last for all of time?
Do you believe what it says is true?
Well I'll let you know . . . I do!

Jenna Fletcher (12)
Ballymena Academy

THE ROMAN EAGLE

A symbol of pride
Or a figurehead of tyranny?
Were the many who died in its name
Heroic fools or foolish victims,
And those who killed for it,
Were they punished for their sins,
Or given a place at the table of their gods?

And is that eagle still so thirsty
For the blood of masses,
That it has changed shape from a bird of prey
To a cross, or a four-armed statue.
Or any effigy in any temple,
That causes people to die for their beliefs?

And were the people who created these images,
In turn, misled by false ideals,
And fooled by dreams of patriotic glory.
Were they wrong?

Fergus Roulston (13)
Ballymena Academy

SNOW

The town was covered in white today,
The snow was all around,
The frost was leaving its evil mark,
Upon the slippery ground.

Children having snowball fights,
Running to and fro,
Snowballs flying everywhere,
Made of crisp, soft snow.

Ladies trying to cross the road,
Slipping as they went,
Cars skidding all over the place,
The air had a wintry scent.

But soon it will all be over,
The snow will disappear,
To be kept away in storage,
Until another year.

Emma Wilkinson (13)
Ballymena Academy

CHRISTMAS

At Christmas the snow begins to fall,
Falling on the trees, roads and walls,
The tall slopes are a favourite place for fun,
Going up and down them until you're done.

On Christmas morning you wake up with delight,
Wondering if Santa had come the previous night,
You get up and wake your mum and dad,
If you wake them up too early they're not too glad.

You see all your presents and smile from ear to ear,
Chocolate and sweets to last you all year,
You eat your dinner but not a sweet,
While you watch the snow fall on the street.

You play with your toys until night,
Waiting until the break of daylight,
Christmas is the time of fun,
The season of happiness has begun.

David Gault (13)
Ballymena Academy

I Remember

I remember you rushing up the town,
 I remember how you never made a frown.
I remember you putting on your lipstick before we went out,
 I remember how you never used to shout.

You never went to bed without your wee hair net,
 And anything I wanted, you would get.
You always met people and stopped to talk the minute we got
                                                  out the gate,
 One day on the way home I counted over eight!

When I was young I used to watch you get your hair permed,
 I used to sit on the seat and wiggle impatiently like a little worm.
You were always so proud of me,
 And every day at ten, you would try to fatten me up by giving
                                         me biscuits and tea!

You and I, we used to skip,
 And over the gate one day I did trip.
You quickly sat me up on the chair,
 Then everything was OK because you were there.

I can remember one day you got sick,
 I prayed to God you would get better quick.
I knew there would be a day we could never see each other,
 As you were diagnosed with cancer later on that summer.

I couldn't hold the tears back,
 I felt so hurt and guilty like I needed a real big smack!
As the summer flashed by,
 I couldn't bear to see you suffer so much I would cry.

We never lost faith and every night I prayed,
   Until one morning I woke up to find it was too late.
I know you're always looking on me,
   I would just love for the last time to say, I love and miss you Granny!

Jamie Anne Wallace (14)
Ballymena Academy

THE DARK HORSE

The midnight bell tolls
From the church on the hill,
The village is dormant,
All is silent and still.
No one to witness
The wicked black head,
Ebony body,
And the feeling of dread.
With fiery eyes sparking
And a wild screaming neigh,
The Dark Horse gallops
On its terrible way.
Looking for its victims
To capture their souls,
Living on the energy
Gathered of old.
But time soon runs out,
The dawn will soon be here,
And no unsuspecting mortals,
No scent of fear.
The rose tinted sky
Signals the dawn,
The hoof beats are silent,
The Dark Horse has gone.

Rachael Ramsey (14)
Ballymena Academy

HALLOWE'EN

Fireworks explode, bright colours drifting like cobwebs into the night.
Witches cackle, banshees scream as you hold your bed covers in fright.
Ice on the roads, the car slides and skids,
Carve some pumpkins, light candles and put on the lids.

Scurrying home to rake up the leaves,
Wear a warm coat or you may freeze!
It gets dark early with a mystical full moon,
Dreading the thought that winter comes soon.

Conkers and beech nuts fall on your head,
Then critters collect them to get ready for bed.
Guy Fawkes reigns on his bonfire throne,
Burning away slowly, without even a groan.

Horses stand, their breath mists in the freeze,
Looking forlorn, with manes ruffling in the breeze.
Hallowe'en is magical, mystical and eerie,
A bright spark in a season that is rather dreary!

David McMaster (12)
Ballymena Academy

ALIENS

Do aliens really live on planet Mars
Looking down on us to see what life's like on ours?
Long and skinny with spindly big toes,
No hair on their head not even a nose.

I wonder what these alien creatures eat,
Sheep, cow or maybe even donkey meat,
Human feet, eyes and toes,
Really in truth no one knows.

Do you believe in aliens and their UFOs,
With their bright green skin which in the dark glows?
I believe in aliens green from head to toe,
Every night I wonder when they're going to show.

Jonathan Mark (14)
Ballymena Academy

TIME

Time is a very mysterious thing,
We schedule our lives to the clock's ring.
It passes on quietly oblivious to man,
But yet is needed to keep our lives working to plan.

Time never stops, or changes its speed,
Time rearranges while we pay no heed.
Time tells us how long the world has been around,
And looks to the future, when life on Mars may be found.

Time is the past, all the episodes of history,
Time is the present, a recurrent mystery.
Time is the future, a progeny of the past,
Time is forever, and long may it last.

Time opened with Genesis, fresh and new,
Time flows past and escapes, beyond our view.
Will time end with an apocalypse, disastrous and frightening
Or will it survive, this age of enlightening?

Time is told by a clock hanging on the wall,
Ticking repeatedly, in a perpetual call.
Time is a strange thing to comprehend,
Transient as it seems, and yet . . . never to end!

Alan Clarke (12)
Ballymena Academy

DAVID MOORE

David is a Chinese-eating kind of guy.
A 'Do you need a hand eating that?'
Kind of guy.
A
    baked potato
    apple tart
    sausage roll
    chippy
Kind of guy
He is a
    mathematician
    geologist
    scientist
    rugby playing
    football playing
Kind of guy
A
    'How you doin?'
    'Hurry up!'
    'Give me a hand!'
    'You're OK.'
Kind of guy
He collects
    PlayStation games
    money
    work
    calls you by your nickname
    and is a champion
        rugby player
        football player
        runner
        comedian
        and friend

He is someone
who
would give anyone
his last chip.

Matthew Young (12)
Ballymena Academy

THE BATTLE

The forces lined out on that cold winter's day,
Looking for revenge swearing, 'Those others will pay!'
The aim of the battle was for power and for wealth,
The leaders not caring 'bout their poor soldiers' health.

The battle 'tween North and South soon began,
North, the larger, held the fort with its land.
All day South's gallant knights did charge,
And the foot soldiers with their battering rams did barge.

Soon the cornfields were stained a pale red,
As many soldiers lay motionless, dead.
And as the day wore on it began to come clear,
That the North would soon lose their castle, so dear.

North's King, badly injured, lay down on his bed,
Then in burst South's knights, the King was now dead.
North's few survivors were soon chased away,
On the South's most victorious and glorious day.

Of the North few escaped injury - if any,
The survivors scarce, the dead were now many.
Their soldiers' faces were scarred and forlorn,
On that terrible, bloody, cold winter's morn.

Richard Wallace (13)
Ballymena Academy

CHARIS ARMSTRONG!

Charis is a box full of chocolates, sort of friend!
A 'Do you want a hand with anything?'
Kind of friend

A
    Crispy chicken
    Chicken gravy
    Crinkle-cut chips
    Chocolate cake
Kind of friend.

She is a
    Chocolate eating
    Hockey playing
    Homework doing
    Dog walking
    TV watching
Kind of girl.

An
    'Are you alright?'
    Always there
    Need some help
    'You'll be fine.'

She collects
    Chocolate wrappers
    Sweet papers
    Funny jokes
    And Winnie the Pooh stuff
    And is a champion
        Hockey player
        Chocolate gobbler
        Giggler
        Tree climber
        A friend

She is someone
Who
Would never jeopardise
Her friendship!

Kerry Aiken (11)
Ballymena Academy

HALLOWE'EN

The nights are getting darker
Hallows Eve is creeping near,
Evil spirits come to life
Generating panic and fear.

The children are getting ready
Their costumes lie in wait,
Little do their parents know
The dangers of this date.

Witches waiting patiently,
Their broomsticks by the door,
Black cats lurking
Evil to the core.

Zombies rise up from the grave,
Roaming the Earth once more,
Werewolves hunt their victims
Causing their blood to pour.

Beware of these immortal beings
Don't stop and pay the toll,
Stay clear of the darkness
If you value your soul.

Laura Featherstone (13)
Ballymena Academy

THE WORLD

The world is a weird and wonderful place,
And we the inhabitants are a sophisticated race,
The world has so many wonderful things within,
And yet we abuse this place we live in.

We the humans that dwell on this planet
Have gone from prehistoric to invent the world internet,
We are the oldest and most dominant species throughout,
The dawn of time to the sun burns out.

The world used to be one united country
Until some ambitious people fought against their adversary,
Thus they separated the world into different regions
From South America to the United Kingdom.

The world itself has many different wonders
Like volcanoes, earthquakes, lightning and thunder,
There are others less dangerous than a volcano's lava walls,
Like the Grand Canyon and Niagara Falls.

To us the world seems so extensive
But yet up in space it seems so diminutive,
If a black hole happened to come by
It would suck in the Earth as easy as pie.

We still have a lot about the Earth to learn,
Yet a fact that comes into concern,
Is that we know more about the moon's face
Than we know about our own Earth's ocean base!

Jonathon Waddell (12)
Ballymena Academy

AUTUMN

The summer's gone,
The autumn is now here,
The leaves turn brown,
The sun disappears.

The nights get dark,
The sky turns grey,
The days get cold,
No one's out to play.

Hallowe'en is coming,
It's time to 'trick or treat',
Children go out to scare
All the people they meet.

Costumes, masks and lanterns,
'Money' in the pies,
Everyone is looking
For witches in the skies!

Squirrels in the garden,
In and out the gate,
They're collecting nuts and berries,
It's time to hibernate.

Winter's round the corner,
The snow's not far away,
Children wrap up nice and warm,
If they want to play.

Deborah McGuckin (13)
Ballymena Academy

HALLOWE'EN NIGHT

On Hallowe'en Night
When the moon is just right,
All wicked witches roam the skies
With their pointed hats,
And their big black cats
They hunt for children all night long!

On their broomsticks they go,
To their haunted home
And in their cauldrons they stir
A piece of a rabbit's fur,
With a few frogs' legs
And some smelly old fags.

Hallowe'en Night will nearly be gone,
In an hour it'll soon be dawn
And as the sun begins to rise
The witches say their goodbyes
Back to their graveyard they go,
As Frankenstein meets them with an unwelcoming
Boo!

Sharon Davison (12)
Ballymena Academy

WHY?

Why do people argue
Over meaningless little things
Like food and television
And future queens and kings?

Why do people argue
Over friends and race and church?
It really gets me thinking
That our lives can't get much worse.

Look at the world we were given,
What sort of mess have we made?
The arguments and all of the fighting,
My hopes of happiness fade.

Everyone should get a chance in life,
Not to be blown to bits by a gun.
All we can do is hope and pray
For peace in the years to come.

Lorraine Fleming (13)
Ballymena Academy

HUNTING

Early Saturday morning we have to rise and shine,
We have to be at the master's house for hunting at nine.
Lots of people gather together,
We load up the hounds and hope it's good weather.

As the hounds run around,
The followers walk along the ground.
When the hounds finally smell the scent of a hare,
They chase it all the way back to its lair.

When we've had enough country air,
We go back to a house and have a cup of tea there.
Everyone thanks the master for a wonderful day,
And that they hope to see him next Saturday.

The hounds are then tired and want to be fed,
And once they have eaten go to sleep in their bed.
They have enjoyed their day running around,
And now they are sleeping not making a sound.

Alex Megarry (12)
Ballymena Academy

My Puppy

My puppy is so full of fun,
I play with him each day.
He loves to jump and skip and run,
And loves to roll in hay.

My puppy often chews the mat,
Which makes Mum very cross.
Sometimes he will chase a cat,
To let it knows he's boss.

My puppy wags his tail with glee,
And loves to learn new tricks.
He sits and begs and gives a paw,
And yuk! My face he licks.

I love my puppy very much,
I know he loves me to.
He's my best friend and buddy,
In everything we do.

Kathy Michael (11)
Ballymena Academy

Rough Sea, Calm Sea

The angry waves come hurtling in,
Towards the beach they crash.
Spray rises high into the air,
Against the rocks they bash.

Small boats are bobbing in the gentle bay,
The waves today they twirl.
A vision of serene tranquillity,
Content for now to whirl.

I love the sea no matter what,
Sullen or sweet its mood.
To stand and gaze with admiration,
Either way is good.

Alison Moore (12)
Ballymena Academy

MY RUGBY MATCH

We arrive in a bus
To a school that is new,
There's a lot of fuss
About how we will do.

We enter the changing rooms,
There's a horrible smell,
How we will do,
Only time will tell.

After we're changed
We run onto the pitch,
We have to stretch
Or our bodies will hitch.

Once the game has finally begun,
I know it's going to be close
Because one of my friends has made a run,
And scored right under the posts.

The final whistle goes,
That's the end,
This match wasn't hard
As we won 51-10.

Patrick Harper (13)
Ballymena Academy

HELL ON EARTH

This is a day that will never be forgotten:
Planes wreaking havoc from the skies,
People running in all directions trying to
escape the gushing inferno,
Clinging to windows, holding hands
and ringing mobiles,
Crumbling buildings like tin cans
being crushed,
Black dust invading the city
like a wild stampede,
Terror everywhere, sirens blaring,
victims screaming
in a city of trauma,
Thousands killed, vanished without trace.
All for nothing firemen risk their lives
Searching through rubble, looking
for answers in a dead end road;
And we all ask why?

Myles Hanna (14)
Ballymena Academy

DAYDREAMING

In history class I sit
In total and utter despair,
Who could have known it'd be so boring
And soon a new world I start exploring.

As I head up through the clouds
I begin to feel more cheerful,
As further and further I go
I'll have lots of fun I know.

As I play football in Old Trafford
I score the winning goal,
I've saved the team from relegation
But this is only in my imagination.

Then I hear the lunchtime bell,
Brought back down with a bump,
But I know that next time I feel bored
There will be lots more to explore.

Andrew Moore (13)
Ballymena Academy

THE BIG SCHOOL

T is for timetables, teachers and talk.
H is for history and hectic homework.
E is for English, oh how I love English.

B is for bells, buses and big boys.
I is for information, we get lots of that.
G is for games, that is my favourite subject.

S is for being a small fry again.
C is for cooking and cold mornings at the bus stop.
H is for homework and home time 'Oh great!'
O is for organising yourself before you are late.
O is for the order, which is maintained through the school.
L is for Latin, languages and listening and back to being
   the little fish in the big pond again.

Nathan Hodge (11)
Ballymena Academy

LISA-JANE MILLAR

Lisa-Jane is a weird kind of friend.
A 'Are you in a funny mood.'
Kind of friend.

A
    Roast chicken
    Cream potato
    Splash of gravy
    Fruit cocktail
Kind of friend.

She is a
    Artie smarty
    Television crazy
    Giggly wiggly
Kind of friend.

A
    'I'm in a giggly mood'
    Always happy
    Boy crazy
Kind of friend.

She collects
    Scary stories
    Chocolate
    Clothes
    And is a champion
        Smiler
        Giggler
        Friend
        Cheese eater
        And chocolate lover

She is someone
Who
Would be anyone's
Friend.

Charis McNabney (11)
Ballymena Academy

THE BOX IS IN CONTROL

The television is just a box,
Lifeless and without motion,
Until a person comes along
And addictively pushes the button.

All at once it comes to life,
Different voices as the channels flick,
The thing in charge is not the person behind the remote,
But the TV itself.

Each channel battles it out,
Trying to intrigue the viewer's attention,
Some channels fill heads with rubbish,
Others important information.

Neighbours, Coronation Street, Emmerdale,
They are all the same - addictive,
The television is a drug,
One with long term consequences.

One minute it's just a box -
The next - it is alive,
Turning heads, making ears prick,
The box is in control.

Sarah Kernohan (13)
Ballymena Academy

WILSON

My best friend is a raw carrot kind of friend
A 'Do you want a sweet?'
Kind of friend.

A
    mashed potato
    sausage, beans and chips
    Maltesers fan
    Mars fan
Kind of friend.

He is a
    great entertainer
    constant laugh!
    champion player on the PlayStation
    adventure man
    video watcher
Kind of friend.

A
    'What do you want to do now?'
    'Want a sweet?'
    'Want to come over to my house?'
    'Are you alright?'
Kind of friend.

He collects
    friends
    good times
    inventive ideas
and is a champion
    at speeding up days
    being a real friend
    tree climber
    weight lifter
    and squash player

He is someone
who
always has a
great time.

Jonathan McLean (11)
Ballymena Academy

THE DOWNHILL RACE

Sitting at the start gate, feeling nervous,
The starting lights are out of service.
People are watching . . . I'm starting to scare,
I wonder why I'm doing this and why life isn't fair.

The start shouts, 'Go!' I pedal like mad.
The spectators are shouting, 'Come on lad.'
My arms start to get sore from all the bumps,
And I have to watch out for stupid tree stumps!

Crash! Bang! Smash! Bash!
Broken bones, maybe whiplash,
Get back on! Pedal! Off the drop!
Turn, jump and a quick bunny hop.

I'm near the end now, not far to go,
I'm starting to think my tyre pressure's too low.
Last steep section . . . hang on tight.
I can see a large crowd watching as I come into their sight.

I go through the finish line, the announcer says my name,
'I fell off again,' I quickly exclaim.
'It was a good run,' she replies,
'Maybe you'll win the worst crash prize!'

Russell Kerr (12)
Ballymena Academy

AN ALPHABET POEM

A valanches of snow pouring down the mountainside.
B ats, flying mammals in dark places, where they hide.
C heese melting on a piece of toast.
D affodils blowing gently by the coast.
E ye, the organ of sight.
F irefly giving off phosphorescent light.
G argoyles, water from their mouths flowing.
H ot coals on a barbecue glowing.
I nferno, a raging fire full of power.
J aponica blossoming with a red flower.
K oalas feeding lazily on a gum tree.
L adies languishing for a shopping spree.
M umps, a virus causing painful swelling.
N eanderthals in Stone Age dwelling.
O asis, welcome water in the desert sand.
P atchwork quilt made by hand.
Q uestions always asked in school.
R aindrops in winter feeling cool.
S addleback pigs wallowing in the mud.
T offee to tantalise my tastebud.
U lster coats made of rough cloth often with a belt.
V arnish, a liquid coating that does not melt.
W alls of Pisa lying at a slant.
X ylem found in the stem of a plant.
Y eti, the Abominable Snowman from it run.
Z any a comical person full of fun.

Brian Millar (12)
Ballymena Academy

AMERICA'S DOWNFALL

Boom!
A cloud of smoke,
A ball of fire,
The crumble of the Twin Towers falling to the ground,
People running,
People screaming.

Inside employees jumping out the windows
Rather than be blown into a thousand pieces.
Others try and run to safety
But have nowhere to run to.

Their families wonder where they are,
What they are doing,
Will they come home tonight,
Or are they dead?

Everyone around the world
Wonders what sick person would plan this,
Kill thousands of innocent people?
Will he be brought to justice?

But I tell you
If he isn't brought to justice in this lifetime
Think of it like this,
He is suffering in his mind
And will suffer somewhere not on Earth,
Where his punishment will be much worse.

Louise McGivern (12)
Ballymena Academy

THE LAND OF JUSTIFIED CRIME

There was a land where crime was right,
What we could call sin happened day and night.

It was the opposite of the land we know,
You could be convicted for saying 'hello'.

Terrorists were welcomed, thieves enjoyed fame,
The people didn't care, it was all just a game.

Until the last night it met its fate,
People tried to stop it but they were too late.

And now it's not there that land of legal crime,
For it has been devoured by time.

Garrett T Bell (12)
Ballymena Academy

FIREWORKS

Fireworks come in all shapes and sizes,
And make bangs and pops and lots of loud noises,
They look colourful and bright and fill us full of delight,
And make pets frightened on a cold dark night.

Fireworks can be dangerous as well as being fun,
And so in the wrong hands can lead to killing someone,
So when it comes to lighting a firework some night,
Leave it to a grown-up who knows their safety rules right.

And when it comes to that Hallowe'en night,
When the stars are twinkling bright,
You must remember your safety rules,
But not to forget the great sight of fireworks high in the sky.

William Fleck (13)
Ballymena Academy

AN ANGEL ABOVE

He told me that he loved me and it helped me through,
And now that he's gone I just don't know what to do,
He was my strength when I was weak,
My voice if I couldn't speak,
God took him for a reason I'll never know,
God took him from me; it was his time to go,
Chris had served his purpose, done what he had to do,
Maybe I'm on my own now but he still lives on in me,
He is still here although he is out of sight,
Shining through the darkness, he is my guiding light,
He was our angel and God took him away,
He has left this world, but is in our hearts to stay,
It is time to say goodbye now and let go of our love,
It's time to start healing now he is an angel above!

Katie D'Arcy (13)
Ballymena Academy

CALENDAR RHYME

In January strong winds blow.
February does not come in slow.
March brings out the pretty flowers.
With it April brings the showers.
May is getting brighter
And June is getting lighter.
July is very fun,
With August's hot, blazing sun.
September, the months are getting colder.
In October the leaves are getting much older.
In November our cheeks start to glow,
While December brings in the snow.

Rebecca Sweetlove (11)
Ballymena Academy

Rachel Rainey

My best friend is a chocolate kind of friend.
A 'Would you like a piece of chocolate?' friend

A
    soft mint
    Fanta lemon
    chip and gravy
    chocolate biscuit
Kind of friend.

She is
    very sporty
    very smart
    good at maths
    and good at art
    listens well
    and kind at heart
Kind of friend.

A
    'Hello there!'
    'Want to play?'
    'Come outside'
    'Are you OK?'
Kind of friend.

She collects
    friends
    teddy bears
    CDs and videos
    posters

And is a champion
    laugher
    sweet eater
    friend
    singer

She is someone
who
would give anyone
her last Milky Button.

Jenny Surgenor (11)
Ballymena Academy

HALLOWE'EN

10pm on Hallowe'en,
Vampires, werewolves and ghosts are keen,
So you'd better get all that you want in the day
Because at night one second is all you'll stay.

And if you try to go outside
There is no use wherever you hide,
Because with that big werewolf's nose
A statue you will have to pose.

But if all that is pretend
Then maybe it is not the end,
But then again it *is* Hallowe'en,
So whatever you do just don't scream.

But there's another side to Hallowe'en that's great,
With toffee apples, pumpkins and even a date,
So if you're not into these ghost like things
Then have a party with us till late.

So is Hallowe'en magic or myth?
Well you just don't know until you've had a whiff,
But if you have you shouldn't tell,
Because if you do in the woods you shall dwell.

Philip Harshaw (13)
Ballymena Academy

Rugby

On Saturday mornings I come to school,
My friends think I must be a fool.
The reason for this is our headmaster
Thinks it will help us learn rugby faster.

Out on the pitch we all have to go,
In rain and wind and sleet and snow.
They say it will help to harden us,
So we must do it without a fuss.

Throwing, passing, running and all,
These are the things we must do with the ball.
These we must do each Saturday morn,
Sometimes it all seems very forlorn.

But to end this tale I'll have my say,
This rugby's a game I like to play.
It isn't as hard as it may seem,
Perhaps I'll even get into a team.

James Bond (11)
Ballymena Academy

My Papa!

My papa was a brilliant man,
Who loved the smell of sausages in the pan,
He always helped me in every possible way,
Throughout every single night and day.

He always teased us until we were bright red,
He was the funniest man I always said,
He listened to what we had to say,
And I miss him from day to day.

He loved going to different places,
Like Asia, Cuba and the local races,
He enjoyed life, that was easy to see,
I just hope I've some of his characteristics in me.

Clare Bamber (12)
Ballymena Academy

MY FUTURE

Now and then I sit and think
About what I would like to be,
A pilot or an engineer,
I wonder if that's really me.

Perhaps I could be a lawyer
Arguing about wrong and right,
Or maybe I could be a boxer
Standing in the ring to fight.

A sportsman would be an idea,
Fame and fortune go with that,
Perhaps a footballer or a cricketer
Playing with ball and bat.

Maybe I should go and study
Then I might become a preacher,
But then that might not suit me,
Perhaps I should become a teacher.

But then I really start to wonder,
My thoughts wander here and there,
I know that sometime in the future
I'd like to be a millionaire.

Adam Bond (12)
Ballymena Academy

GOLF

On those lazy summer days,
There's nothing that I'd rather play,
Than my favourite sport called golf,
It's just something that I really love.

The deep blue ponds reflect the sun,
But when your ball falls in, it's not much fun.
You're walking near a river and you see a lost golf ball,
You run down to get it, careful not to fall.

You hit the ball the best you can,
And in the hole is where it should land,
If you're bad and hit a slice,
If someone got hit it wouldn't be nice,
To stop this happening any more,
It would be best to shout:
Fore!

Craig Barr (11)
Ballymena Academy

THE SEASIDE

The warm sun shines,
A refreshing breeze sweeps by;
Some people swim, others sunbathe,
A few build sandcastles.

The waves roll towards the beach,
Their white crests dancing;
Strands of seaweed edge towards the shore,
Only to be pushed out again.

The cold sea water swirls around my ankles,
Deeper; waves break gently against my shins,
Being splashed and sprayed by the sea,
What else is there like this?

Hannah J Simms (12)
Ballymena Academy

YESTERDAY'S FIRE

I sit alone in the early hours
Looking at the fire's still, grey ashes,
With the odd red coal glowing through the blanket of grey ash
Like winter aconites peeping through the snow.
And I think of a few hours earlier
When the fire was in its majesty,
Roaring up the chimney like a ferocious caged beast
Greedily demanding more fuel,
Eating up the oxygen, commanding where people sat,
And being such a focal point.
Suddenly, a small puff of gas shoots up from the ashes,
Surrounded by flame, reaches up high, like a miniature firework,
Looking for something to grip onto, but there's nothing there
To keep it alive.
I gather together my thoughts of the day,
The day that had just disappeared like the fire.
I gently rake through the ashes,
And let them slide down, through the hot iron grate,
Grey ashes spangled with sparks, like small rubies,
Their smoky scent lingering in the room,
Soon what was once a glowing mass of wood and coal
Would be reduced to a pan full of useless ash,
Gone forever, just like the day that has passed.

Clare Kennedy (12)
Ballymena Academy

ANIMALS

The mouse runs quiet to the cheese,
The rabbit eats the carrot gnawing its teeth,
At the moonlight the wolf howls,
And the brown fluffy cub growls.

The rampage of a boar,
Makes the tiger roar,
And so does the sound of a hunter's gun,
It also makes the antelope run.

The mustang graze on a grassy plain,
The eagle soars effortlessly without any pain.
The hare does a leap so beautiful and high,
Whilst the eagle swoops down from the sky.

All these animals will soon be extinct,
And so will many others,
What do you think?

Coral Gardner (11)
Ballymena Academy

IT'S COMING

Short, dark days
Nights spent close beside a fire,
School shuts its doors,
Presents bought then wrapped.

Cards coming and going,
Mum in the kitchen, pots, tins overflowing,
Tree up, with lights ablaze,
All rooms suddenly look changed.

The church at night alight with praise,
I try to sleep, I will the sleep to come.
The house is silent as I waken,
Until I realise it's Christmas Day, hooray.

Robin Adair (14)
Ballymena Academy

HELLO - GUY FAWKES NIGHT!

Bonfire Night is a night to remember,
Falling on the 5th of November,
Monday to Sunday the night doesn't matter,
Celebrations made to make our nerves shatter!

Hallowe'en's been,
We have all seen
Catherine wheels, sparklers, bangers and rockets,
Children beware danger is there, it's wrong to leave
Them in your pockets.

The night is frosty and without a breeze,
We quickly gather our twigs and leaves,
Arranged in a pile oh, what a height!
We'll have such fun on this special night.

Apple dunking, trick or treat,
Knock on the doors, who will we meet?
Dressing up is fun to do,
Witches, ghosts and devils too.

Gun powder, treason and plot,
Were all Guy Fawkes' lot,
Bonfire Night is a night to remember,
Falling on the 5th of November.

Jenny Patton (13)
Ballymena Academy

SCARY SPIDER

S cary spider in my shoe
C all my dad and he'll soon get you.
A way you go if you can
R un, run oh what a hoot
Y ou've had it now here comes my foot!

S cary spider in the bath
P lease don't touch me dare I ask
I won't hurt you, if you won't hurt me!
D on't dare go into my dad's room or he'll kill you with glee!
E very time I see a spider I just go mad.
R un little spider before you meet my dad!

Erin Russell (11)
Ballymena Academy

INSIDE THE DOLPHIN'S BEAK

Inside the dolphin's beak,
Lots of little fishes,
Inside the little fishes, the coloured coral bed
Inside the coral bed,
The dolphin's mysterious calls,
Inside the dolphin's calls, the current of the sea,
Inside the current, the fluffy, white foam,
Inside the foam, the dolphin's eye,
Inside the dolphin's eye, the starry sky,
Inside the starry sky, the dolphin's prey,
Inside the dolphin's prey, the coloured coral bed,
Inside the coral bed, lies the dolphin and its beak.

Amy Colgan (12)
Ballymena Academy

NOT ME, NOR YOU

So tall, so large,
millions of people passing through every day,
Seven years to build
yet seven minutes to destroy.
The Twin Towers shouted out what man could do
The plane crash also shouted out what man could do.
Thousands alive, now thousands dead,
but who could do this?
Not me, nor you.
But we know who did this -
conscience lies under the rubble with those who died.

Timothy Rocks (12)
Ballymena Academy

I KNOW SOMEONE . . .

I know someone who plays rugby, the great sport,
I know someone who, to his team, gives great support.
I know someone who can be a great mate,
I know someone who plays music really late.
I know someone who loves Ferrari cars,
I know someone who wants to go to Mars.
I know someone who has a good sense of humour,
I know someone who is a mighty consumer.
I know someone who likes Walt Disney's Goofy,
I know someone who featured him on their duvet.
And that someone is . . . *me!*

David McComb (12)
Ballymena Academy

THE SEA AT NIGHT

As a bright silver moon rises high against an inky blue sky -
Still the darkening waves continually crash along the shore.
From the water's edge, to where the sea meets the moon,
The vast amount of shadowy waters slowly become overcast
With the surroundings,
But where a glowing moon is found so high in the sky -
There is not complete darkness . . .

For the moon which shines so clear,
Illuminates the black, mysterious waves.
Creates a path of glistening light -
Along the surface of the sea,
Stretching out and ending where the waterside
Finally meets the shore.

The sound so recognisable, unique and clear.
The only sound that can be heard -
Waves beating against the worn rocks, falling hard upon the shore -
The sea so violent - yet a feeling of calmness,
The noise - loud, with a feeling of silence.
So evident these things all are at night.

Soon the moon lightens,
The distinct sounds become hidden.
The sea becomes still,
And all the astounding details, that are noticed in the dead of the night -
Are concealed and are not uncovered,
Until another night comes!

Kristine Porter (13)
Ballymena Academy

WHAT IS BLUE?

What is blue? The sea is blue,
Where the ships sail through.

What is red? A poppy's red,
In its barley bed.

What is pink? A rose is pink,
By the fountain's brink.

What is yellow? A banana's yellow,
Rich and ripe and mellow.

What is green? The grass is green,
With flowers in-between.

What is brown? A tree is brown,
Growing in the ground.

What is white? A swan is white,
Sailing in the light.

What is gold? A lion's gold,
On the plains so bold.

What is black? Coal is black,
We get it in a sack.

What is violet? Clouds are violet,
In the summer twilight.

What is orange? Why an orange,
. . . Just an orange.

Rachel Swann (11)
Ballymena Academy

THE SEA

The beauty of the sea

The sea is so majestically plotted
And in it the seaweed is carefully dotted.
It makes us think about beautiful nature,
It tells us to get out our sketcher
To draw the most majestic scene,
And show some people where you've been.

The wonders of the sea

There are many secrets about the sea
And some are as tiny as a pea.
It has so many wonders
And we make so many blunders.
Each little, tiny living thing
Has so many details in its swing.
Each wave has its own time
To keep it in rhyme.

The courage of the sea

You know the sea is so daring
Yet with each wave it's caring.
It really can bring trouble you know,
In the winter, rain or snow.
It sometimes could make you worry
When waves come in in a hurry.
Sometimes waves grow high in the night
And then crash in with all their might.
You can often be deceived
And this is where I'll leave.

Emma Logan (11)
Ballymena Academy

DO I HAVE TO GET UP THIS MORNING?

Do I have to get up this morning?
My hair fell off last night,
If I go to school today,
Everyone will get a fright.

Do I have to get up this morning?
My school bag fell in the pond,
The headmaster sold the school,
And a wizard hit me with a wand.

Do I have to get up this morning?
In my sleep I walked into the door,
And when I got back into bed,
My head went through the floor.

Do I have to get up this morning?
The clock landed on my head,
And later when I woke up,
It felt like I was dead.

Do I have to get up this morning?
No one takes my attention,
And I can't go to school today,
Because I got a double detention.

Do I have to get up this morning?
I've got a broken leg,
A monster ate the school,
And I'm sick of eating egg.

Do I have to get up this morning?
The sky fell on top of my head,
It made me feel so dizzy,
And then I fell out of bed.

Rory Smith (12)
Ballymena Academy

WHEN MUM TURNED INTO A TEACHER

When Mum turned into a teacher,
Was the day my life went grey,
Perfect homeworks,
Lots of red crosses,
School right here at home.

'Tuck your shirt in, do it quick!'
Is my morning 'hello',
Eating a breakfast of muesli and milk,
'To keep you going, my dear!'

Watching Number Time instead of Blue Peter,
It is hell with my mum as a teacher,
I do hope that soon,
My mum will be sacked,
For being a fiend of a teacher.

Hooray, the day has come!
No more teacher, only my mum,
She is no more a class-eating mistress.

Aisling Dundee (11)
Ballymena Academy

OUR PLANET

Think of your children, think of the future,
Think of the destruction for which there is no cure,
Once nothing's left, all is gone,
And the only darkness is just from dusk till dawn.

Does anyone ever stop and look as time passes by?
Does anyone ever stop and listen and hear Mother Nature cry?
She's fighting a battle she knows she can't win,
In a world of greed, corruption and sin.

You don't even glance as the world is stripped bare,
You don't do a thing, you don't even care,
Never found cures for cancer and disease,
Do you still think it's just a few trees?

Species extinct, animals lost,
Money for them, but at what cost?
This once beautiful planet, shall never be the same,
And the cold, hard truth is we are all to blame.

Rebecca Stevenson (13)
Ballymena Academy

THE DYING WORDS OF A SHARK

A Stealth Bomber in the sea,
In a world no one can see.
Fish, mammal, coral,
That's what you'll see.

You want me for your soup,
Cut off my fins,
Then you throw me back in.

My mother and father had the same fate,
My time has come.
My grave is rocky,
Cut and sore, soon to die.

It's too late to save me,
Bleeding and drowning!
Now . . . I am dead.

Dale Gallagher (12)
Ballymena Academy

THE FOUR SEASONS

The tall, green shoots stretching, reaching and grasping at the sky,
Like an uncoiled spring springing into life and shooting upwards.
Buds blooming to life giving the tree back its lush green coat.
Trees, daffodils, crocuses and primroses are giving nature colour,
Like tiny rainbows streaking across the countryside,
A riot of colour brightening even the darkest corner.

The kind, warm glow of the sun beating her rays down,
Heating the world like a lightbulb lighting a room with a warm glow.
The beautiful golden sand of the sunbathed beach,
The soothing sound of the water cool and quiet lapping gently,
Against the warm golden sand of the beach like the wind breaking on
                                                             the hillside.
The cold, sweet taste and sound of slurping, licking and sucking
                                                             of ice cream.

Thin, spindly twig-like fingers,
Grasping at their coat of leaves slowly unravelling.
Falling, twisting, turning, swirling to the hard, cold ground,
A gust comes, suddenly hoisted up into the air,
Like a troupe of dancers twisting and turning and swirling,
Before twirling slowly to the ground like a blanket.

Snowflakes falling, twirling, tinkling and twisting,
Down and down eventually resting upon each other,
Like stitches linked together to form a great white blanket.
The crunching as the first robin merrily skips across the frozen grass.
Jack Frost making his mark on the world with his frozen patterns
                                                             of ice,
Nipping at children's fingers and noses with an icy bite.

John Gregg (12)
Ballymena Academy

CRUEL PARTING

Quietly she goes about her daily chores,
Politely acknowledging a passer-by
She steals a quick glance at the time,
Her pace increases, the click of heels
Becoming more definite.

The distant, overhead drone comes closer but
not arousing any unusual thought.
The sudden blast which that follows
Causes her heart to miss a beat.
A low rumble, like a growl rising from deep
in an angered beast's soul.
Her penetrating gaze absorbs the smoke,
Dust, debris, rising above the city skyline.

Still she stands, silently, staring,
Is it true? It couldn't be.
Outside in the world her consciousness has
left, people are in a frenzy.
The visions which cloud her eyesight
Causes fear to settle in her heart.

Her body trembles as his tender brown eyes
enters her thoughts like a sword of ice.
Burning tears stream down, streaking her face.
She knows her life will never be the same
This is the beginning of the end.

Gently the police officer places his arm on her shoulder,
leading her across the rubble; dusty specimens of
terrorism.

Rebecca Dempster (15)
Ballymena Academy

WIFE
(With acknowledgements to Arthur J Lamb)

Her beauty was sold for an old man's gold
She's a bird in a gilded cage.
She's a prisoner of perfection,
Trapped by her delicate rage.

Revelling alone in a glorious home,
Living as an elegant queen.
Obedience, modesty and duty bids
Her not to be heard, just seen.

Her love has died in her pitiful plight,
She is used as a prop in a show,
With her charming smile and dazzling style
To set the party aglow.

Bought for her beauteous presence, was she,
Bought for her exquisite face,
But her enchanting soul is worth more than gold
So she hides it behind a guise of grace.

Shwetha Janarthanan (16)
Ballymena Academy

CHRISTMAS

The snow is falling heavily,
The weather outside is cold,
Santa comes around this time,
Or so I was told.

I've left some apple tarts out,
And a glass of milk,
I hope he gets me a bathrobe,
Made of some pure silk.

Hooray! It's the morning time,
The Christmas tree looks bright,
I look out of the window,
And the snow looks purely white.

I am really happy,
While trying out my gear,
But unfortunately it's all over,
For another year.

Craig Edwards (11)
Ballymena Academy

HOCKEY

Hockey is the sport I like,
You don't need a racquet, club or bike.
But bring a stick, mouthguard and ball
And shin pads too in case you fall.

Eleven players make a squad,
In our kit like peas in a pod.
Goalie, sweeper, right and left back,
Leaves the rest to form the attack.

We play on Astro Turf or grass,
And whack the ball or gently pass.
A tackle sometimes saves the games,
But a winning goal is our main aim.

Hockey is the sport I like,
And I play best when wearing Nike.
It helps my game, improves my looks,
Maybe I'll make the record books.

Joanne Healy (12)
Ballymena Academy

THE AUTUMN FULL MOON

On one autumn night
The moon is full and bright,
It looks like a ball of cheese
In the cool autumn night breeze.

As the night lights up
The wolves begin to howl,
The leaves fall off the trees
And my dog begins to growl.

Travelling along in the car
The moon shines bright,
There are people walking
In the middle of the night.

As dawn is breaking
The moon begins to sink,
Soon it will be forgotten
In a flurry of orange and pink.

Jonathan Davison (12)
Ballymena Academy

BEAUTIFUL ISLAND, GOODBYE

The ground began to shake and rumble
Then my house began to crumble
I ran and then got out
I was leaving without any doubt
I got in my car
And shot off with my guitar
I went round a corner it went out of sight
I turned again with a fright
There it was as large as life
Cutting through my house like a huge knife
The sky turned black

A shadow was cast on my back
I went really fast
I didn't want to be last
I was almost out of fuel
I began to scream like a mule
The island, the Emerald Isle
Turned to an ash pile
The pyroclastic flow coming at 100 miles per hour
I got out of my car
My friends drove by
Beautiful island, goodbye.

Adam Gault (12)
Ballymena Academy

SPACE

A world of difference,
A world of silence,
A world of peace,
A world that will never cease.

As the thousands of galaxies
And the millions of stars
Glitter so brightly in the moonlit sky,
I often ask myself - how?

A vast openness,
That has lain unexplored
And probably will for all eternity,
Far beyond the reach of man.

A universe of beauty
Without disturbance,
That I wish I could explore,
But can only dream of.

Christopher Patton (12)
Ballymena Academy

THE WAVE

The day is dull, the rain is lashing violently upon my head,
The air is cold, it hits me like a knife,
I look out to sea,
I hear the smashing roar of waves as they hit the land,
I feel the madness, the chaos of the sea as I stand and stare
I go for it
I run, then dive into the cold, bleak darkness,
I begin to paddle out,
An avalanche of water powers its way towards me,
What do I do?
Go over it? No, go under.
I fill my lungs with the wintry, bitter air,
As I take the plunge, I feel the pandemonium above.
I bring myself to the surface of that deep, dark ocean,
The roaring of the sea has stopped, it is so calm.
But wait: there is something on the horizon,
What is it?
It speeds faster and faster,
Another wave in its swell is hurtling towards me,
I turn myself, begin to kick frantically,
There is no turning back now.
It catches me and throws me forward.
The wave begins to break,
I slice through the water speeding along the chaos,
The wave forms a bridge over me,
And the white water chases me.
It can't catch me but I know it wants me,
I can feel my heart thumping faster and faster,
Smash! The wave sucks me under,
I can't get out! I'm tumbling with no control,
Thud! I hit the sand and the terror stops.

Ben McQueen (14)
Ballymena Academy

IAN

My friend is a chips kind of friend
A 'Can I have a bun with my crisps?'
Kind of friend.

A Chips
    Brown gravy
    Crisps
Kind of boy.

He is a
    Sit on the couch
    Watch TV
    Eat
Kind of boy.

A
    'Have a snack'
    Always lazy
    Greedy
Kind of boy.

He collects
    Fat
    PlayStation games
    And is a champion
        eater
        TV watcher
        and sweet chewer

He is someone
who
wouldn't give anyone
his last sweet.

Alistair Black (12)
Ballymena Academy

A DAY OF HORROR

What is that?
A plane?
Why is it so low?
Bang!
Workers scream and shout,
Hanging out windows,
And even jumping.

What is that?
A plane?
Why is it so low?
Bang!
Another one?
More screaming,
And now crying.

Help, help, they shout
One tower falls,
Silence,
Shouting again,
By this time the whole world knows,
Silence around the world,
In shock.

The other tower falls,
Rubble left with injured people,
Searching but no sign of life,
Many citizens mad but sad,
Is this war?

Adam Shingleton (14)
Ballymena Academy

A JOURNEY

It may be early but I'm wide awake,
I will not miss this by waking up late,
The sun has not risen,
The birds are still asleep,
I've packed my bags,
Well, my clothes are in a heap.

I'm in the car,
I'm grinning all over
The journey has begun,
The sun has passed above the trees,
The birds are singing,
The air is sweet.

My body aches,
My eyes are stinging,
I've had no sleep,
And I haven't been eating.

My legs are numb,
I'm bored out of my mind,
'No! I won't play I spy one more time!'
'Are we nearly there yet?'
I feel like crying.

I'm too tired to be excited,
Too hot to even care,
Too sore to have some fun,
I'm so glad we're finally there!

Nikita Strange (15)
Ballymena Academy

ENTOMBED

As I lie here, in the dark, dusty ruins,
I remember my family.
Do they know?
Do they know how much I miss them?
Want to talk to them?
If only for a few minutes,
Just to say goodbye.

I can hear the faint call of voices,
But I am too weak to reply.
My body aches,
My eyes are heavy.
What happened?
An earthquake? A tornado?
Was this planned?

Flashes go through my mind,
Going over yesterday,
Walking towards the door,
Then opening my eyes,
Finding myself trapped amongst the rubble,
So lonely and scared,
So helpless, so lost.

A small ray of hope washes over me,
A mobile phone, lying within arms reach.
I pick it up with what little strength I have left,
Punch the numbers 911, then the call button,
Only to hear the message 'Battery Empty'.
The phone clatters to the ground,
With a last soft sigh
I close my eyes.

Diane Wilson (13)
Ballymena Academy

MY FAVOURITE SPORTS

Rugby is my favourite,
I play it Saturdays.
I run and tackle,
Score and cheer,
My team forgets *fear!*

Golf is my favourite,
I play when I can,
I drive and putt,
Straight and true
And sink it in the *hole!*

Table tennis is my favourite
I play on Friday
I serve and hit
Smash and score
I never hit the *net!*

Football is my favourite
I play it with my mates
I dribble and pass
Shoot and score
And never miss the *net!*

Swimming is my favourite
I swim when I can
I dive and bomb,
Splash and float
And never, ever *drown!*

Matthew Wilson (12)
Ballymena Academy

JOEY DUNLOP

Joey Dunlop was 'King of the Road',
Both at home and abroad.
Ballymoney was his hometown,
His racing never let him down.

Joey owned a small bar,
He went to race near and far.
Joey had a big white van,
He was known as 'Yer Man'.

Joey was not one for the limelight,
Just to stay at home for the night.
Linda was the name of Joey's wife,
Who always supported him through his life.

His helmet was bright yellow,
Joey was a quiet fellow.
Going down the road at 120mph he had no fear,
As he passed the fans they gave him a cheer.

When he won a TT race,
Joey was a super ace.
When he was in a race,
You could see the determination on his face.

Alan Graham (12)
Ballymena Academy

SCHOOL!

We get in right on time,
Get our books and be there for nine,
Meet our friends, have a laugh,
Next we know it's time for class.

First it's Latin then RE,
I wish I had a cup of tea,
Ah! Off we go to break at last,
Run, run, run, we must be fast!

Two more periods then it's lunch,
Something nice to crunch and munch,
I hope there's money on my card,
Otherwise I might get barred!

Home economics is such fun,
Making all those sticky buns,
Washing up is not such a treat,
It's usually such a massive feat.

Hallelujah, it's time to go,
There's the bell, let's not be slow,
Once outside we're free at last,
But the weekend sure does go fast!

Alison Craig (11)
Ballymena Academy

AUTUMN

Gold, brown, red and green
Dancing around in the wind.
What do all these colours mean?
And where have they been?

Dark nights, shorter days
The fresh feeling in the air.
People coping in different ways
The fire bringing them hot rays.

This season bringing Hallowe'en
Fun and flames, dressing up and games.
Fireworks sparkle orange and green
Every flare wanting to be seen.

The apples gone from the trees
Gathered away safely.
Empty branches now swaying in the breeze
Everything in a deep freeze.

Cold days, shorter too
Colours of rustic hues.
Nights of blue
All of this to do with autumn and you.

Carole Addis (11)
Ballymena Academy

THE MOUSE!

My mum gave me some money,
To buy myself a treat,
She said it could be anything,
(as long as it wasn't sweets).

So off I went to spend it,
I wandered round the shops,
I couldn't find a thing,
When something made me stop.

There in the pet shop window,
I saw a little mouse,
I gave the shopkeeper the money,
And took it to my house.

When my mum saw it,
She jumped up on a chair,
She said, 'Get out! Get out!'
And started to pull her hair.

My mum gave me some money,
To buy myself a treat,
She said it could be anything,
(as long as it was sweets).

Andrea McGuigan (11)
Ballymena Academy

I Cannot Go To School Today

I cannot go to school today
My throat is burning red and grey
My brain has stopped
My bed is nice and cosy hot.

I cannot go to school today
50 lines I'll have to pay
And if tomorrow they don't show up
Death and destruction will turn my way.

I can't be bothered to go today
My teacher's hair is turning grey
Her eyes are blue
Her cheeks are red
And when she's mad she bangs her head.

Stewart McKee (13)
Cambridge House Grammar School

Leaves

The leaves fall off the trees,
All of the colours mixed together,
Red, green, orange, brown and gold,
Flying about in the breeze.

They move as if they're dancing,
Or children playing games.
Suddenly they stop,
And fall to the ground,
Where they stay
Until once again they're blown away.

Karine Carleton (14)
Cambridge House Grammar School

WINTER

Now winter is here and Christmas is near,
Mistletoe and tinsel, snow on the window sill

There is no hot sun but we'll have lots of fun
Playing in the snow, that's me, Emma and Flo

Santa is coming and my mum is running to and fro,
So fast she nearly broke her big toe

I ask her, 'What have you got?'
She says, 'Not a lot!'
I know she won't tell me so I ask my sister Dee;
'Wait till you see it under the tree!'

I love this time of year
Now winter is here.

Ashley King (13)
Cambridge House Grammar School

CATS

Ginger, black or tabby,
Moggies never look shabby.
Sitting in front of the fire,
Gently cleaning herself,
But then ever so quick, she's dashed up onto the shelf!
Kittens race and hardly ever fall,
The proud tomcat stands tall,
Waving his bushy tail high up,
Then hissing at the noisy pup.
They run, they play, and then they sleep,
Silently in the corner, not one peep.

Kathryn McNeilly (14)
Cambridge House Grammar School

AMERICAN TRAGEDY

The day the world stood still,
6000 souls were lost at what
the eye could count,
their families grieved for them in
disbelief.

As the metal bird crashed, the
devastation was still to come,
not only souls were lost but
money, time and effort, as the
bits of rubble fell.
Devastating could not describe
that day, all hearts fell.
The air was filled with shock
and terror,
onlookers watched with tearful
eyes in sorrow.

The world was filled with sadness,
the city of New York will never
be the same.
Why did this happen?

Davita Duff (14)
Cambridge House Grammar School

AUTUMN

We know that autumn has arrived,
The trees are losing their leaves,
Blowing and twirling down to earth,
They are not fussy where they dived.

The wind's started off with a gentle blow,
Before you know, it's more than a blow,
Next it's whistling for all its worth,
Strong and cold must come from the north.

All of a sudden from bright to dark,
Cloud slinks over and lets a crack,
From dry to wet in the blink of an eye,
The rain drove down, is there need for an ark?

Michael Steele (14)
Cambridge House Grammar School

THE LOST CHILD IN THE TOWN CENTRE

Town centre is a busy place,
All car parks full with no parking space.
People looking and wandering all around,
Clarifying to family and friends what they have found.

My child stay close by my side,
And don't go off to hide.
Tugging and pulling Mum by her hand,
Dragging her into HMV to find her favourite pop band.

Mum, Mum buy me S Club 7!
No Cher, we have to pick up Kevin.
Come along Cher or we'll be late,
No, I won't cause it's you who I hate.

One minute here, one minute there,
I've lost her, it's not fair.
Oh child, oh child come back,
I promise I'll treat you with a Big Mac.

In and out the shops, wandering with fear,
Over my darling dear.
HMV, I'll check one more time,
Surprise, surprise, she's fine!

Gillian Rainey (13)
Cambridge House Grammar School

WAR

The world is dark and gloomy
Men with bloodstained clothes
Children crying and men dying
Bang, bang, bang in the night
Aircraft flying overhead
Bombs being launched
Massive craters being made
With fire breaking out
While others starve
Men in camouflage come to kill
Not just enemies but the innocent too
Whole nation's fate in one man's hands
Then it is launched
Whooshing through the sky
Then in a flash it drops
A bright light appears
Blink and you would have missed it
An awful noise hitting you
While the ground vibrates
And a giant mushroom appears
Millions dead, total destruction.

David Stewart (14)
Cambridge House Grammar School

THE WIND IS LIKE A LION

The wind is like a lion,
They lie down low and hide,
And then spring up and surprise you,
When you're least expecting it.

The wind is like a lion,
They both are strong and wild,
They're fierce when they want to be,
And can cause serious harm.

The wind is like a lion,
And whenever they get tired they back down,
It's as if they die away,
Until another time.

Gillian Millar (13)
Cambridge House Grammar School

SCHOOL

With the babbling fools
And the scary ghouls
That come from library books
I write this poem from my detention desk
Listening to teachers scold.

With decimal points and multiplying
Maths is even worse
The weird sounds that come from tubas
Will wake the dead.

The burnt food from cooking class
Tastes as bad as it smells
The PE hall stinks of sweat
Because the PE teacher can't afford deodorant
Because of his low salary.

After all I've said
There's still one thing you need to know
And that's
I love school.

Daniel Cummings (11)
Cambridge House Grammar School

FROST

There's frost on the window
There's frost on the door
When you look around
There's frost on the ground.

There's a nip in the air
And the trees look very bare
But little Robin Redbreast
Doesn't seem to really care.

The pipes are frozen
The water won't run
No time for dozing
Except you're the sun.

The frost looks like icing sugar
That's been sprinkled in the night
But if you go to take a lick
The chances are your tongue will go numb.

People wrapped in warm clothes
Some grey and very old.
For then the summer months will come
But not before Jack Frost has gone.

Leanne Kernohan (13)
Cambridge House Grammar School

POP STARS

I wish I could be a pop star
To tour the world in a chauffeur driven car
To live life in a hurry
Without a care or worry
With managers to pay the bills
While I have all the thrills.

To always look my best
And perform like all the rest.
After all the supportive bands
To hear the cheer of all the fans
You know what I mean
But a girl can only dream.

Jenna Maxwell (13)
Cambridge House Grammar School

THE WAR

What are you supposed to do during a warm,
Sit and watch the devastation and destruction?
The unfortunate women and children,
Who lose their loved ones in the duration.
All I ever see is depression and sadness
In this orphanage.
All the shouting and bangs,
The shooting of guns and loud voices.
I can't sleep thinking of all the lives
That have been taken away.
Some people die a slow and painful
Death of starvation.
The missiles that take away all
Those innocent lives.
The men who risk their lives
Fighting to save the country.
Trying not to let the other side
Take away their pride.
I just sit and wonder if
The end will ever come?

Adrian Nicholl (13)
Cambridge House Grammar School

SCHOOL

School is very boring,
I could fall asleep snoring.
All those yappy teachers,
They are always on your back.
All that work gives sweating palms,
And tests are even worse.
And as the bell rings, it's break time,
And Mr Love is in the house.
Gorgeous girls are always around
Till the bell rings at half-past ten.
It's back to class
And you're there in a flash,
Hoping you're not too late,
Or extra work you'll have to have.
My brain is going to burst
I'm working so hard for the first
But that won't last too long
As the bell rings
It's the end of school
And back to bed it is.

David Meeke (13)
Cambridge House Grammar School

THE SPIDER

Spiders are insects, they have no wings
They look like little evil things
Big and small, different colours
Put on Earth to frighten mothers.

The widow is black
With red on her back
She can kill
And some day will.

The spider spins its tangled web
Like a fisherman with his net
Trying to catch wandering souls
Before the evening sun can set.

David Torbitt (13)
Cambridge House Grammar School

LOST

The wind howled as I ran through the wood,
The trees shook with the wind,
I was lost.
I stood in true horror,
I saw a dark shadow,
I ran.
I couldn't see,
The light of a car blinded me,
It shone with great brightness,
I was trapped.
I couldn't go anywhere, do anything,
Something crept towards me,
I was terrified.
I was even more horrified,
I saw another light flickering,
I ran towards it.
It seemed to get smaller and smaller,
A dark shadow loomed close by,
It was a man.
I ran to him,
He helped me out of the wood,
I was grateful,
I was safe.

Simon Jamieson (11)
Cambridge House Grammar School

AT MIDNIGHT

At midnight when the moon is out,
And the wolves are about,
People get scared,
And scream out loud.

At midnight when the air is cold,
And the clouds are low,
Owls' hoots are heard by one and all,
As animals scuttle about below.

At midnight the breeze is light,
And all the shops are closed up tight,
Burglars are about to give you a fright,
When you wake up in the morning.

Gareth Marcus (12)
Cambridge House Grammar School

THE COLOUR RED

My favourite colour is red,
Just like my Uncle Ted's,
My dad likes his bright red car,
The only thing is, he drives too far.

I have a bright red bicycle,
The same as my brother's tricycle,
I always win when we race,
But it's sad to see my brother's face.

My dad wears a bright red tie,
He says he's happy, which is a lie,
But, I think it's the best colour of all,
Bright and posh making you stand tall.

Mark McLean (12)
Cambridge House Grammar School

Dolphins

To me you are an inspiration,
You really are a true sensation.
Your graceful ways
Always bring pleasure to my days,
As you play amongst the waves.

Your talents are endless,
Your actions are fearless.
You have such a good feature,
Which is why you're such a beautiful creature,
As you play amongst the waves.

Your skin is smooth, as smooth can be,
Watching you brings me such joy and glee,
And that is why you never cease
To amaze me,
As you play amongst the waves.

Daena Lipsett (14)
Cambridge House Grammar School

Autumn

Autumn is the time of year
When some of the trees shed a tear
Some are red, some are brown
But they all flutter to the ground
It's the time of year for witches and brooms
Gunpowder plots and fireworks' fumes
Trick or treats, money or sweets
Shout the children as they roam the streets.

Ross McKervill (13)
Cambridge House Grammar School

HOMELESS

Each morning I walk down the street,
I pass you by at my feet,
You live so far, but yet so near,
To all other people your life is a drear.

Your memories are many, your possessions are few,
Each day you wake up to the wet, winter dew,
To others your future is clear,
Which you know, you and I both fear.

I always throw you a coin or two,
But even still your life is full of woe,
Your life is hard, it's not fake,
For that you have all my respect.

Deborah Storey (13)
Cambridge House Grammar School

SEASIDE

Waves are splashing
People are dashing
Down to the sea today

Grabbing their boards
Running in hordes
Down to the sea today

The sun is away
We had a great day
Down to the sea today.

Kristopher Orr (13)
Cambridge House Grammar School

MY NEW SCHOOL

Scared and frightened,
   Lots of eyes staring at me,
Saying 'Aww! Look at the wee first years,'
   Trying to get to their next class.
Getting squashed at either side,
   My legs trembling and shaking,
My face as white as a sheet,
   Meeting new teachers, nervous and shy,
My heart beating at 60 miles an hour,
   The bell rang, I jumped,
Finally it was over, I was home at last.
   Then I remembered,
I had to do it all over again tomorrow.

Lindsay Forsythe (11)
Cambridge House Grammar School

WINTER

In winter the snow lay all around
like a great white rug covering the ground.
In gardens stood snowmen big and small,
some looked sad, some happy, but still I liked them all.
I tied my scarf around my neck,
the frost was nipping at my nose,
and I didn't really mind that I could barely feel my toes.
Just then *Splat! Giggle,* it was my friend Paul
who found it rather funny when he hit me with a snowball.
As the day was over, and I went in for my tea,
I was very, very happy, because I love winter you see.

Glenn McGivern (11)
Cambridge House Grammar School

THE SMALL BROWN FOX

There's a small brown fox across the street
I see it every night.
Sometimes I try to approach it,
But it runs away,
When I'm in sight.

Last night I saw it hunting
A helpless field mouse.
It ran across the road,
And entered my neighbour's house.
I heard her screaming out,
'Get out, get out, get out.'

As I listened to the racket,
The fox had run away,
But it was sure to be back again,
To catch its doomed prey.

And sure it was
The fox came back,
To have a feast that night,
And caught that mouse
With a gruesome and unforgiving bite.

The fox had won the battle
Between itself and the mouse
And ran away in victory,
To share its prey with its spouse.

Andrew Thompson (14)
Cambridge House Grammar School

FREE KICK

Juggling the ball like a magician
Running down the wing,
When *Boom!*
He's brought to the ground,
The referee blows the whistle
Reaches for his pocket
Revealing the yellow card
He places the ball on the spot,
Poised to thunder it into the net
Will he miss?
Will he score?
Silence! Fills the stadium
As he hits the free kick.

Gary Pollock (12)
Cambridge House Grammar School

CALENDAR RHYME

In *January* strong winds blow,
February does not go in slow.
March brings out the pretty flowers,
With that, *April* brings the showers.
In *May* the days are getting brighter,
In *June* the nights are getting lighter
July is a lot of fun,
Next comes *August's* hot sun.
September, the months are getting colder,
October, the leaves are getting older.
In *November* our cheeks start to glow,
While *December* brings in the snow.

Lauren Tennant (14)
Cambridge House Grammar

WAR POEM

The soldiers lying in the bunkers
Some falling to their hunkers
The guns are firing
Some soldiers are getting shot
The enemy killing without a thought
The army tank is coming
All the soldiers are running
All the bombs are flying
And everyone is dying
People dying of disease
They are rationed to eat peas
Everyone is devastated
All the buildings will need to be renovated
People dying because of depression
They're going like evaporation
If anyone was caught
They were taken away and shot
Put the gas masks on
The siren has gone
The soldiers wait till dawn.

Andrew Lindsay (14)
Cambridge House Grammar School

FAME

Fame is everybody's aim,
It's all in the name,
Just a glamour covered game,
And your life will never be the same.

People think it's the way to be
But if only they could see
It's not all glitter and money
Or big car and living in places sunny.

Yeah, it's full of great treats
But I'd rather get a video and a bag of sweets
That way you always know who you are
Instead of some shallow star.

Simone Forgrave (13)
Cambridge House Grammar School

WAR

War is like a mushroom cloud,
It grows more menacing by the minute.
A bomb goes off,
as the fires rage.
A soldier dies,
the guns are firing.
Disease spreads,
as the flags fly half mast.
The submarines can't be seen,
as the heavy aircraft fly above.
The president is distraught,
as the destruction continues.
The tanks roll in,
as the evacuees scamper out.
People search for gas masks,
as the thick smoke is unbearable.
War brings death,
in many countries.
The colours are bursting,
and the soldiers are camouflaged.

Peter Kennoway (13)
Cambridge House Grammar School

WAR

Big ships sail out across the sea
Whilst planes leave airports in multiples of three
Soldiers load their guns with ammunition
Then take up their plotted position
Civilians in the targeted country see
The need to gather loved ones and flee
They rush in thousands from the city to the border
All to escape this inevitable murder
Planes drop bombs, ships send missiles
Devastation reigns over many miles
Weary war-torn soldiers lose their will to fight
The only way out is to commit suicide
A lucky few are taken home by Red Cross
But many of our comrades are forever lost
The futility of war is seen all around
Whether it be terrorism, religion or a bit of ground
There's bound to be a way to sort out our quarrels
Without loss of life or compromising morals.

Steven Boyce (13)
Cambridge House Grammar School

FOOTBALL

Football is a sport of joy,
Mostly played by all the boys,
Twenty-two players on the field,
All hoping to succeed.

Ninety minutes of blood, sweat and tears,
All searching for the goal in the net,
And every goalkeeper who makes a great save,
And all the defenders who get the ball cleared.

Every penalty,
Every free kick,
All the chances to score the great goal,
And all the players who made the game look easy.

Jason Steele (12)
Cambridge House Grammar School

THE MATCH

I walked out,
Onto the freshly mown grass.
After 90 minutes,
It went to penalties.
On the fourth strike
We were drawing 4-4.
My heart was pounding,
Sweat trickling off my forehead.
The opposition missed
It was my shot.
I took my position,
My heart still thumping.
I smashed my foot against the ball.
The goalie dived,
Crashing onto the ground.
The ball slammed into
The back of the net.
The stadium roared,
I had scored.

Gary Crawford (11)
Cambridge House Grammar School

THE MOTORBIKE RACE

The 3 beeps at the starting line,
3-2-1
And I was off,
I felt the shaking of the engine,
As I flew round,
Lap after lap,
Never first, always second
And then the opportunity arose
The leader had stalled
I sped past him
And then victory was in my grasp
4 laps to go 3 . . . 2 . . . 1,
As I turned on the final straight
The engine failed
Smoke billowed from it
The line was within metres
I had lost my chance of success
The victory was taken away from me
I hated the bike
I hated the race
I needed to win
But I had lost
And standing on the podium where I should be
Stood my rival who had won
The whole championship was lost
All because of my stupid motorbike.

Michael McMaster (14)
Cambridge House Grammar School

FIRST DAY NERVES

Beep, beep, beep,
Beep, beep, beep
The alarm clock goes off,
It's the end of my sleep.
Uniform on, new shoes on my feet
Kiss Mum goodbye,
My heart misses a beat.

In through the door
Where I've not been before
New shoes on my feet,
Are making me sore.

New faces, new places
Don't know what to do
Is everyone else going through this too?

Different subjects, different classrooms
So much more to remember.
At least five more years of this,
And it's only September!

One day, one week, one month
It soon passes,
After a while I remember my classes.
And if I work hard along with the masses,
I hope to get my GCSE passes.

David O'Neill (11)
Cambridge House Grammar School

THE WINTER EVENING

The winter evening settles down
With a gradual silence descending on the
Vacant streets once filled with last minute shoppers
Darting from one shop to the next, attempting to escape the icy chill
That nips at their skin and numbs their fingers.

People scurry home to toss their precious parcels carelessly aside,
To participate in a more fulfilling and rewarding pastime.
Pans rattle, steam spews out through open windows
As a thousand different aromas fill the air . . .
And then . . . silence.

This golden but short-lived silence is rudely broken
By the insane babble of television sets
As people settle down for the night to relax and unwind
From the stress and pressure of their hectic lifestyles
To the peace and tranquillity of the winter evening.

Rachel McLaughlin (17)
Cambridge House Grammar School

FIRELIGHT

F is for flames as they spread so wide.
I is for igniting flames as they jump so high.
R is for rage the fire releases upon us.
E is for embers, smouldering and smoking.
L is for licking at the coal.
I is for igniting sparks smoking as they go.
G is for glowing embers in the grate.
H is for hot which the fire is.
T is for trouble that fire can cause.

Hugh King (11)
Cambridge House Grammar School

F1 RACE

There goes the flashing lights,
Then the noise of thirsty engines.
Speeding closer to the car in front,
Pushing towards two hundred mph
You pass him on the corner,
Some of the crowd cheer,
To see the flash of colour.
Then comes the pit stop
Should you stop or not?
You pull in,
With only a few seconds to spare.
After all those laps,
The race is finally over,
You are the victor.

Shane McMullan (14)
Cambridge House Grammar School

THE CAT

With mossy paws,
And quiet stealth,
She tiptoes along the window shelf.

With graceful ease,
And not a care,
She coils upon the kitchen chair.

With noiseless motion,
She springs,
And is gone,
Through the open window,
Across the lawn.

Judith Erwin (12)
Cambridge House Grammar School

MY FAVOURITE SUBJECT

My favourite subject is PE
My teacher Mrs Henry.
My second is Spanish,
Hola, Buenas noches.

Third is geography
Not technology.
Then there's RE
Followed by history.

Sixth is French,
I always get work wrong.
Next is music,
It's nice to sing a song.

Last is English
Which is no fun.
All we get is assignments,
And this is one!

Jayne McGrillen (12)
Cambridge House Grammar School

A STORMY NIGHT

It was a stormy night,
as she lay in bed.
She had a sudden fright,
when something hit her head.

She put on her light,
and looked at her clock.
It was the middle of the night,
it was twelve o'clock.

As she got out of bed,
she wiped her head.
It was cold and damp,
just like camp.

She glanced at where her head had been,
then looked above at the ceiling.
Why had she got so worried?
It had just been a drop of water.

Nicola McMaster (12)
Cambridge House Grammar School

WAR

The button is pushed
The missile is flying
The opposition is reported
The enemy still smiling
The alarm is raised
The president is told
Then goes on TV
Says, 'We have to be bold.'
The nation is in shock
As millions hear,
'Run for cover
The missile is near.'
The men prepare
The children cry
As the mothers scream,
'Why, why, why?'

Robert Winton (14)
Cambridge House Grammar School

THE DARK

Walking alone in the dark,
Watching the stars spark,
Listening to the wind whistling,
And the leaves rustling,
Suddenly I hear a howl,
Oh, it's just an owl.

I hear the scratching of a mouse,
He is looking for a new house,
I am walking past the field gate,
What is that strange shape?
I hear it snort and shuffle,
Oh, it's just a cow.

Oh, how I hate walking in the dark.

Andrew Colvin (11)
Cambridge House Grammar School

WALKING THROUGH THE NIGHT

Walking through the night I see the moving shadows
What I find, I have tingles down my spine.
Everything I see gets more and more horrid
All I know is I want to get home quick
Before I see something truly frightening.

I start to run but can't get away
Everywhere I go there's darkness
Oh what will I do?
I'm lost and I can't find my way home
What am I going to do, but then I see the light.
I can see my home shining in the reflection of the moon
I'm home, but I was lucky to escape walking through the night.

Samuel Strange (13)
Cambridge House Grammar School

WAR

Bombs dropping from the sky
Torpedoes flying underwater
Stealth plane gliding silently through the sky
Battered bodies lying on the road
Civilians forced into depression
Blood streams through the town
Death hanging in the air
Mushroom cloud roaring in the sky
Fires exploding here and there
Tanks rolling in from everywhere
Armoured troops being blown to shreds
Torn flags flying high
President Bush going wild
Buildings crumbling to the ground
This is why I hate *war!*

Paul Dunlop (13)
Cambridge House Grammar School

HALLOWE'EN!

Hallowe'en is a time of scaring
A time of ghosts, masks and daring!
There are lanterns aglow and skeletons dangling
Witches and shadows and silver chains clanging
There is a werewolf rising from its tomb!
There's a witch on her motorised broom
You ring the doorbell say, 'Trick or treat?'
And if you're lucky, you get something sweet.

Rachel Henry (13)
Cambridge House Grammar School

First Show

I enter the ring on my pony,
Ready for jumping a course,
I heard the speaker start up,
Before I knew we were off.

Ahead of us as I looked,
It was an unsafe stonewall,
I hope Pepi isn't spooked,
It looks really, really tall.

Over a cross pole,
Jumping another,
On comes the rain,
The audience takes cover.

The last fence is the double,
Pepi has no trouble,
We canter through the finishing posts,
And receive the big red ribbon.

Lynsey McFetridge (12)
Cambridge House Grammar School

Bluebells

Purple, blue,
Everywhere I look,
Bluebells.

Beautiful bluebells,
Cluttered together like a blue sea,
Sway in the soft breeze.

Overhead the beech trees dance,
To the sound of the wind,
While green leaves rustle.

As the sun sets,
Everything turns quiet
Ssshhh!

Jennifer Rock (12)
Cambridge House Grammar School

THE KITTENS

As I went out today
I went to the garden to play
There two little kittens lay

On a rug in the middle of our lawn
They were black but mostly fawn.

I lifted them and ran to Mum
Who at that time was eating a plum.

She jumped and screamed
'They may have fleas.'

'But Mum they are so cute and sweet
Please do you have a blanket or sheet?'

All I can see is a tiny little head
I'll have to keep them in the shed

'Mum do you have any food
I promise I'll be very good.'

Sarah Rainey (12)
Cambridge House Grammar School

AUTUMN'S RETURN

The leaves are falling
The wind is blowing
Is that voices I hear calling

Maybe it's the swaying of the trees
But to me it's the spirits screaming help me please!

Maybe it's my imagination getting carried away
But as I listen carefully I understand and hear more
of what they say

Their voices are terribly weak
As they try so hard to speak.
But still I can only hear their mumbles travelling in
the heavy breeze

They go on to say something like
'Have plenty of fear
Hallowe'en's nearly here
But as they begin to start a new sentence their
voices are chucked aside by the wind!
It's now Hallowe'en, soon to be autumn's end!

Danielle Kinney (12)
Cambridge House Grammar School

THE DINNER

I'm in the living room watching TV
My mum calls to me 'Dinner's ready!'
I come into the kitchen as usually I do,
What's on the menu? Could it be stew?

When I sit at the table,
I think, am I able to eat more turnip and peas.
I say to my mum,
'Can't you make anything different please?'

My tummy has just rumbled,
At the thought of apple crumble,
Mum shouted, 'Who's for strawberries and cream?'
'Me, me, me we all scream!'

Laura Livingstone (11)
Cambridge House Grammar School

I'M A BUTTERFLY!

Before I turn into a butterfly
I have to change out of my green skin
Into my brown pupa dress.
I wait patiently, I wonder -
Wonder what colour I'll be.

Perhaps I'll be orange
With black spots
Like a tiger,
Or cream
Like the moon.

As I wake up
From my dream
I realise that I haven't got
A brown shell any more.

Hooray!
I'm a butterfly.
When I work out how to fly . . .
I fly to the lake-like puddle
Down below the tree where I
Changed,
I'm purple and pink
My favourite colours.

Deborah McCracken (13)
Cambridge House Grammar School

AUTUMN

The brown leaf stands alone on the top of the withered tree,
All of its friends have fallen to the harsh world.
The leaf sways left to right as the wind howls and growls past it.
It shakes so hard as if it was trembling at the sight of the fall.

Finally at what sounded as the leaf's last breath the wind blows hard at it.
The leaf finally loses its grip and falls slowly down from the top of the tree.
It flutters about like a butterfly doing somersaults,
At last it hits the ground to no notice of the rest of the world.

The leaf now joins the rest of its friends as the old park keeper sweeps them away.

Richard Patton (13)
Cambridge House Grammar School

BLUEBELL WOOD

Bluebells swaying to and fro,
Dancing gracefully on tippy toe.
Wood anemones peeking through,
Their eyes follow you.
The smell of apples in the air,
Primroses are dancing in a spring fair.
A hungry badger makes a trail,
As the wind tells its tale.
Squirrels jump from tree to tree,
The stream trickles like keyboard keys.

Rebecca Mawhinney (13)
Cambridge House Grammar School

WAR POEM

Up rises the mushroom cloud, it covers land
for miles,
If you're under the acid rain something bad is sure
to happen.

Gas masks can't help you now, once the rain
has fallen,
All you have to do right now is take the pain
and suffer.

Aircraft and bombs can kill thousands, only
some survive.

But after all it doesn't matter, life is sure to end,
Let's just hope we live on to very old age.

Rachael Selwood (13)
Cambridge House Grammar School

DURING THE NIGHT

During the night
When the moon is bright
The wolves will give you a fright
And the owls hunt down their prey.

During the night
When the breeze is light
You really want to sleep tight
And the shadows are dancing high.

During the night
When the bed bugs bite
And the animals scatter about
You really want to *shout!*

Jason Stewart (12)
Cambridge House Grammar School

HALLOWE'EN

Hallowe'en is a time for fun, lots of treats for everyone,
Lots of folk enjoying themselves despite the scary goings on,
Hallowe'en's a bright colourful time of year,
Bright coloured fireworks and sounds in your ears.

Brown and crispy leaves are found,
Tricks or treats are all around,
Weird and wonderful costumes, even big kids dress up too,
Lots of sweets and tasty food for everyone.

Down the street they're having a party,
Each one's preparing for the kids to come,
Hustling and bustling to get their sweets and treats,
Each home is decorated, the spookiest one's at the end
                                          of the street.

Now comes the patter of feet rushing down the street,
A knock at the door or a ding-dong on the bell
Is the next thing to be heard in our house,
Open the door and all you can smell is the seasony smell,
Then come the fireworks roaring and whistling and
                                          flashing across the sky.

Now comes the big question . . . Trick or treat?
What shall we choose?
What do you think?

Jonathan Boyd (13)
Cambridge House Grammar School

A FOGGY NIGHT

A grey mysterious stranger,
Draped her veil around the town,
Enveloping all in sight,
Muffling all the sounds.

A single set of dipped car lights,
Approached the stranger's veil.
Unable to venture further
Retreated in the silence of the night.

Lyndsay Williamson (16)
Cambridge House Grammar School

THE MYSTERY MAN

He drives a red car
As fast as a rocket.
He drives through the roads,
And never goes home.

He comes to my school,
Five days a week.
He walks down corridors,
And he walks upstairs.

He wears a raincoat,
Down to his feet,
And the tie he wears,
It's down to his knees.

He'll never say hi,
Or goodbye.
If you say hi he'll just,
Walk on by.

Who he is remains a,
Mystery.
But until I know he'll remain,
The mystery man.

Kathy McCarte (12)
Cambridge House Grammar School

THE SEASON CALLED AUTUMN!

The golden brown leaves swiftly fall,
Slowly and silently,
To the leaf, littered floor,

Red, brown, orange and yellow,
The leaves' colour changes,
As does the weather,

To the longer nights,
The colder days,
Windy gales may soon be coming our way,

So wrap up tightly,
In your hats and scarves,
So the warmth can soon be ours,

Autumn's not too hot or too cold,
So go on out and enjoy it,
While it's here,
Because it's the best season of the year!

Rebecca Hanna (11)
Cambridge House Grammar School

NIGHT

When the long winter nights close in
It's all still and quiet
With not even a peep of a mouse
Or the rustle of a leaf

When the grey misty nights begin
It's all dark and silent
With not even one little sudden movement
Of a twist in the air.

The winter's sky,
Lit up by the twinkling stars
Shining and sparkling
Through the night.

Megan McCaughan (11)
Cambridge House Grammar School

THE WRITER OF THIS POEM

The writer of this poem . . .
Is as small as a mouse
As happy as the sun,
As warm and kind as a house.

As quick as lightning
As bold as pink shorts,
As clever as anything
As strong as army forts.

As cross as a bull
As funny as pie
As boring as school,
As bright as the sky.

As stubborn as a mule
As fast as a cheetah,
As silly as a fool
As tasty as pizza.

The writer of this poem
Even though she isn't tall,
Her personality isn't small
(Or so this poem says!)

Ruth Barr (12)
Cambridge House Grammar School

DON'T BE AFRAID

An abduction of aliens,
Flying up in space,
A snow of yetis
Bite off your face
Bands of banshees,
Get on your case
A blood bank of vampires,
Love how you taste
A bandage of mummies
Are a pile of old waste.
A graveyard of skeletons,
Haven't invented toothpaste.

A moon of werewolves,
Love a wee bite,
A host of ghosts,
Can't stand the light,
A pest of poltergeist,
Are out of sight.

A grange of giants
With a big appetite
A theatre of phantoms
Will make you go white
And a march of monsters,
Always parade through the night.

Ricky Hood (12)
Cambridge House Grammar School

MUSHROOM CLOUD

M is for many
U wanted missiles
S winging through the sky
H is for the hideous death with the
R ed blood all around
O ur feet and lots of
O ur relatives have been killed by the
M issiles when it

C rashed
L oudly into the sea
O nly VIPs able to get into the
U nderground shelters, not a lot of us.
D is for dreadful deaths.

Selina Shingleton (14)
Cambridge House Grammar School

NEW YORK...

N ever before have we felt such fear.
E veryone has shed a tear.
W eep little children for parents lost

Y ou have suffered so much at a high cost.
O ur thoughts and prayers, sadness and grief
R eligious fanatics beyond belief
K eep us all safe from the terror unknown.
                    New York, New York
                        You are not alone!

Victoria McCartney (12)
Cambridge House Grammar School

I Have A Wish

I have a wish
I wish for peace
I have a wish for happiness
I have a wish for equality
I have a wish for freedom

I wish that my wishes all come true
Maybe not in this life maybe
But some day some way they will

If you had a wish what would it be?
Think wisely now for this is your chance
Think of war
Think of the starving
Think of the sick
Thing of the poor
But most of all think of peace

If you had a wish what would it be?

Katy McAllister (13)
Cambridge House Grammar School

A Bit About Me!

My name is Vanessa
I am quite sporty
I hate chicken curry
And I'm far off forty

I love little animals
And I've got a little dog
My sister got a gerbil
And we wouldn't like a frog

I am quite sweet-toothed
As I love Miniature Heroes
My favourite is Fuse
Although I like Cheerio's

I have to go now
I hope you know more about me
And I hope you enjoyed this poem
And did I mention I like tea!

Vanessa Wilson (11)
Cambridge House Grammar School

SPORT

I like sport

The thud of a tackle
The swish of a ball
The screams of the players
The smack of a fall

The whiz of a runner
The swoop of a glider
The stealth of a hunter
The splash of a diver

Many sports are really fun
So take your pick choose any one
There is no sport that can't be done
Practise hard you'll be number one

So now you see
I like sport.

David Millar (12)
Cambridge House Grammar School

HORSES

Horses are the most wonderful things God could have put on
                                                         this earth.
They run about and jump and shout
But you wonder what it's all about,
They laugh, they sigh
And I'll tell you why,
There're free they say
All the way,
From you're on their back until
Taking off tack,
They cough and splutter
Because they've got a stutter.

They run in the fields to make you laugh
To let you see they're as wonderful as,
A bee, a tree and the sea,
A dog, a cat and a flying bat,
A rabbit, a mouse and a house,
And all other things like that.

Lyndsey Montgomery (11)
Cambridge House Grammar School

FRED

My dog Fred,
Loves curled up in bed.
He'll watch the telly,
As you rub his belly.

My dog Fred
Is as cuddly as my ted.
What he likes most,
Is to eat your toast.

My dog Fred,
Has a clever little head.
He listens as you talk,
Great! It's time for a walk.

Kathryn Young (12)
Cambridge House Grammar School

WILL WE MOVE FORWARD?

Switching seats, adjusting the mirrors,
All in preparation for take-off.
Turning the key, hands at ten to two,
Always remembering, 'ABC from the right,'
Accelerator, brake, clutch.
Foot to floor, into first, handbrake off,
Will we move forward?

OK, try again, but more concentration,
Which adds to the frustration,
Moving off gently, 'More acceleration!'
Splutter, jolt, just about made it.
Into second up to twenty,
Into third, up to thirty.

'This is too fast, we'll never get stopped!'
Thank goodness for dual control.
Into second, down to twenty,
Into first, down to ten.
Brake gently, clutch in and stop.
Will I ever move forward?

Emma Bamber (17)
Cambridge House Grammar School

WAR

War is deep and dark fear,
Where no one dares to interfere.
Bombs and missiles go east and west,
While children in schools hide behind their desks.

The President gives orders,
As soldiers flee to front lines.
Wives depressed,
Eating less and less.
Starvation sets in, as disease spreads.
Men lying in rotten streets dead.
Army tanks roar,
As fighter planes soar.

Destruction everywhere is all I see,
As my eyes fill with water just like the rain.
Who started this war, I want to know?
My family are dead,
And I'm all alone.

Naomi Millar (14)
Cambridge House Grammar School

HAUNTED

Graveyard in a forest,
Robed in ice,
Spine-chilling, eerie, hair raising,
Church bells peal,
Full of fear, I jump.

Nicola Gillespie (11)
Cambridge House Grammar School

WAR

War is missiles falling to the ground.
War is that dreaded sound.
War is the mushroom cloud.
War is very, very loud.
War is people fighting.
War is fires lighting.
War is a small child crying.
War is someone dying.
War is destruction all over the world.
War is bombs being hurled.
War is shelters being built.
War is Osama Bin Laden's guilt.

Pamela Livingstone (14)
Cambridge House Grammar School

WAR

People are dying of hunger and disease
The rations are in short supply for all those who need them
Men are hiding everywhere with suits of camouflage
The army do their very best to try and save their country
But some things don't go as all the people planned
Buildings crumble to the ground as the bombs hit them
People running frantic looking for family members
Borders are closing down so the evacuees camp as close as they can
People are really depressed from all that has happened
Why does it have to be like this?
Can they not work out some other plan?

Carolyn Adams (13)
Cambridge House Grammar School

The Horse

The horse starts to gallop through the rich, green meadows
As it gets faster the wind begins to blow through its mane.
Its clean, chestnut coloured coat has a brilliant glow
                                as the sun shines on it.

The foal trails behind its mother, trying as hard as it can to keep up.
As the horse gallops further into the meadows, it disturbs
                                the peaceful countryside.
It scares the birds out of the trees as it swiftly moves by,
Its powerful legs making a thud as they hit the ground.
Its tail swishes back and forth as it turns to come back.
It looks behind to check the foal is still in view and is following.
As it comes to a halt it gazes over the fence with its
                                chocolate brown eyes,
Wishing it could be in the outside world.

Gayle Armstrong (13)
Cambridge House Grammar School

Peace

Violence, what's violence?
I heard a child say.
Guns and weapons were nowhere to be found.
Religion was not a problem,
And nobody cared what you looked like.
The streets were spotless,
And not a homeless person to be seen.
Then I woke up,
It had all been a dream.

Katie Crooks (11)
Cambridge House Grammar School

SEPTEMBER MORNING

As I wake up and greet the morning
I am amazed by what I see
The world is crimson, russet, saffron
The leaves so prominent against the steel grey sky
I climb onto the bus and make my way up to school
The world rushes past full of golden splendour
I wander along taking in all that's around me
My feet crunching in the leaves that litter the ground
A shrill bell cuts through my daydream
And I quicken my pace
I join the crowd, fighting to get through
I feel trapped, suffocated by the crush of people
And wish to be back outside.

Kelly Anderton (15)
Cambridge House Grammar School

WAR

War is the missiles flying from space.
War is the depression on the soldier's face.
War is the mushroom cloud that fills the sky.
War is the bunker where the people lie.
War is a race to destroy one another.
War is the sadness when a child loses his mother.
War is the destruction all around.
War is the bodies as they fall to the ground.
War is the disease that follows after.
War is a time without any laughter.

Lauren McMaster (13)
Cambridge House Grammar School

THE FACULTY OF LIFE

In a world full of different cultures,
So many people are full of vivacity,
How sick, how sad and how naive.

It began at birth.
Pleasant - beautiful - innocent and calm
And before we know it
They can crawl,
Then they walk and there the trouble starts.

Then came that mutant metamorphosis
They call the teenage years.
It's peer pressure you see
First the lethal cylinder, followed by a joint.

She went from moral to immoral
From hilltop to valley bottom
And there at the bottom she finally stood.
How sad it was to dabble with the lethal cylinder and the joint.

They in purple robes who reign on high,
Did not care about her, to them
She is but another, in a long line of hopeless, 'vagabonds'.

It's known as the Faculty of Life.
Who really cares about us?
Birth, toddler, teenager and then adult - it's all a journey
There at the end we will meet the Alpha and the Omega.
In the Faculty of Life, we learn to love, to dance
And to rejoice with humble hearts -

Let this be a lesson - learn to dance and to rejoice with heart,
Think of they who have failed this life - there they lie aside - drugged
No hopes and no dreams.
Surely all life is a faculty of learning?
With winners and losers and tossed our hearts?

Jim Caldwell (16)
Cambridge House Grammar School

WHEN THE NUKE STRIKES!

The nuke it struck the land
It sounded just like a thunderstorm
Until I saw the astounding light
Which you would think a blind man could see.

The ground, it started to shake
It rocked, so strong, so fierce.
The earth cried out in a rumbling moan
With more than a thorn on its side.

The feel of the air, so hot
Hotter than the hottest fire.
A blast so strong it did level
Many a factory, a house and a shop.

Warm rain it came down and caused havoc
Carried radioactivity it did
Anything in its path contaminate
Leaving hardly a drop of water to drink.

Now a pinkish glow it has left
Hardly a survivor in sight can I see
Each man for himself we are now.
Leaving one thing on my mind but to live.

William McKee (14)
Cambridge House Grammar School

LIFE

Each day we wake up, blinded by the sunlight
through our curtains.
The sun, the moon, the stars, we take these all
for granted.
Never did we think that these could be taken away
in one split second,
but that is life.

We walk down the street - skyscrapers, shopping malls
and people.
These could be wiped away in one fell blow.
Devastation, fire, death, we know too well.
But that is life.

Life is like a hungry shark hunting its prey
ready to pounce.
Death is another feature of life people tend to forget
but it comes to loved ones when unexpected
and that my friend is life.

Alison Millar (13)
Cambridge House Grammar School

DON'T QUIT

When things go wrong as they likely will
Sometimes life is all up hill,
You feel discouraged and discontent
The burden weighs like a tonne of cement.

Life is strange with its twists and turns
As everyone of us sometimes learns,
Yet sometimes failure turns around
If we have got our feet firmly on the ground.

Don't give up though the pace seems slow
A glimmer of hope may come with another blow,
Success is failure turned inside out
That's what life is all about.

You can never tell how close you are
It may just be over the hill or far,
So keep on fighting the battle when hardest hit
It's times like this you must not quit.

Patricia Boyd (12)
Cambridge House Grammar School

IT CAME LIKE A LION

It came like a lion
Silent until its prey was in touching distance.
First it unleashed a blinding flash,
After that came the shaking,
Shaking so violent it made you quiver
From head to foot.
The radioactive dust was the next
To rear its ugly head
Covering and contaminating
Everything it ran its fingers through.
After that, there was a sudden hot blast
If you were not dead already,
You are dead now.

The Grim Reaper appeared to many a person
The day the lion came to call.

William Wilson (14)
Cambridge House Grammar School

SPECTATOR

People are dying,
Missiles are flying,
Submarines glide,
Bombs by their side,
Headed for who knows where,
Perhaps for Bin Laden's lair,
Starvation is creeping,
Among those all weeping,
Evacuees headed,
For new homes they've dreaded,
Soldiers are fighting,
In the cold so biting,
Perhaps the cold will kill,
More than the fighting will,
Who knows?

Alison Arnold (14)
Cambridge House Grammar School

WAR

How did it start? No one knows!
Bombs, guns and missiles all rose.
The aircrafts in the sky, the ships in the sea
Help before I become an evacuee.
All I can see now is disease and starvation
My mum has been taken away because of depression.
The soldiers with their gas masks on and
their suits full of armour.
The boss of it all must be a real charmer.
All I can see now is blood and dying
Someone make it stop and all the crying!

Amanda Gaston (13)
Cambridge House Grammar School

FOOTBALL

Sitting watching the football
It's on every TV channel.
Michael Owen they all call
As their team runs from the tunnel.

David Beckham calls for tails
The match has now begun.
England vs Wales
The players off they run.

The 90 minutes are nearly up
Michael Owen scored
England has won the World Cup
Oh how the crowd roared!

Helyn Rankin (13)
Cambridge House Grammar School

THE HORSE

His long muscular legs carry him
Swiftly through the once peaceful countryside
His silk body shines in the glistening sunlight
The gentle breeze runs through the strands of his smooth mane.
When he grows tired only then will the countryside be quiet
and peaceful again
When the dark night swallows up the sun
At dawn he will take to his travels to his favourite part
of the country
And the peaceful countryside will be awakened
By the sound of his thudding hooves.

Ruth Knowles (13)
Cambridge House Grammar School

WHAT WAS ONCE OUR TOWN

War is . . .
The look of depression on a child's face,
The soldiers marching at a steady pace,
The president saying that all will be fine,
Although a war is not a good sign.

Fire flying everywhere,
A mushroom cloud darkens the air,
People starved and begging for food,
Evacuees at the station stood.

A parent cries at the loss of her child,
While meantime the bombs go off like wild.
The women stand crying, with tissues in hand,
As their husbands head off to fight for their land.

The deaths have gone up,
The bombs have come down,
War has destroyed what was once our town.

Julie Whann (14)
Cambridge House Grammar School

WAR!

I'm sitting here in the cold breeze
The air is over and I have the disease.
There's lots of people in this town dead
But more are wanting to be fed.

I'm waiting for the ship to come
When I hear a sound like a bang of a gun
I'm glad that I am out of here
Because I am full of terrifying fear.

I can't even laugh at the Prime Minster
His jokes and laughs are far to sinister
I really hate Osama Bin Laden
I'd like to see him nice and flattened.

The war is full of different colours
With lots of blood and crying mothers.
I see a massive war plane coming
I've got to go now and start running.

Sarah Robinson (13)
Cambridge House Grammar School

DRAGONS

There was a gust of wind,
A clap of thunder.
Dragons rumbling way down under.

A terrifically bright flash of light
That filled my head with fear and fright.

The ground was shaking
So strong and fast,
A burning feeling of a *very* hot blast.

Bits of rubble fell on my head,
I was choking,
People were *dead.*

Then there was silence,
A pinkish glow,
The dragons were still rumbling,
Down below.

Sarah-Kate Goodwin (14)
Cambridge House Grammar School

A Rude Awakening

I stroll along the bay of a secluded, desert island,
I can feel the hot sand
Gently filtering through my toes, grain by grain.
The sun is like a huge, glittering orb,
Reigning down on me from the vast cloudless sky
And its relentless heat overwhelms my senses.
The salty air penetrates my entire body
And the ocean beckons me to its glassy waters.
I can hear the distinctive sound of the albatross,
Swooping down on the lush vegetation,
Searching for the delicious taste of that unknown fruit.
Suddenly a large shrilling noise,
Disrupts my haven.
My eyes are opened and I am quickly reinstated,
To the real world,
As my alarm clock has already told me so.

Paula Kerr (16)
Cambridge House Grammar School

The Winter Evening

The winter evening settles down
With howling winds and beating rains
Leaves drifting from off the trees
And an icy chill is setting in.

The winter evening settles down
A flick of a switch, a burst of noise
As events unfold and news is told
Devastating, shocking and seasonally bleak.

The winter evening settles down
An aroma drifts, a feast prepared
And savoured with each bite, then
Only 'Thanks dear, that was nice.'

The winter evening settles down
A roaring fire lit, crackle, spit
A gathering place to beat the chill
And moan and mull over life and love.

Linda McCord (16)
Cambridge House Grammar School

A LETTER FROM VIETNAM

Dear Mom and Dad
I write to let you know I live
Though I don't know for how long
Khe Sanh village was attacked
The base and our gear is gone.
Now we are living in bunkers
Like the marines at Con Thien last fall
My body is weak and bleeding
And I have no hope at all.
My buddy was killed yesterday
He caught a piece of shrapnel in the head
A mortar hit his bunker
Half of our company is dead.
How could our great country
Get us into this mess?
I feel like an old man waiting . . .
Waiting for death.

Nicola McFall (17)
Cambridge House Grammar School

MOTHER AND DAUGHTER

The connection between the two,
Some would describe as inseparable
The protective nature of the mother,
Shielding what seems to be her only possession
Away from prying eyes.

They are more than two creatures,
They are now one
As their love for each other unfolds.
As every second, minute, day passes
The bond grows deeper.

Together they can achieve anything,
Alone they are transfixed
By thoughts of the other.
This relationship is based on trust and love,
This love will last forever.

Lucy McGaughey (14)
Cambridge House Grammar School

THE CAT

Sitting in a window chair,
A young girl focuses her attention on a cat.
A golden leaf falls from the tree,
But she continues to study the black feline,
Watching as the crisp leaf
Caresses the animal's slim structure.
The creature does not stir.
It carelessly sits peacefully,
Looking ahead wide-eyed, the cat moves
And swiftly strides off out of sight.

Louise Penny (15)
Cambridge House Grammar School

IN THE MEADOW

The elegant horse stands tall and proud
Her mane blowing in the wind,
Her coat shines like silk
In the blazing sun.

She gallops across the open field
Trotting swift and free,
Gracefully, only stopping once
To groom her clumsy foal.

They lie together lovingly
In the dappling shade
And so they dally there
Until the sun disappears behind the trees.

Michaela Beattie (12)
Cambridge House Grammar School

WAR

Why is there war,
Is what I want to know
Do we detest each other that much?

Enough to kill, to shed others' blood,
In hope of maybe being free
As countries are blown up
And nations destroyed.

When will it stop, or will it ever?
As we blow up our world and people lives
We hope and pray that we might see our
Stupidity and give peace a try.

Alyson O'Flaherty (14)
Cambridge House Grammar School

TRAPPED

The class quietens down
I let my mind wander
I hear the constant drone
Of cars as they drift down the road
I stare out the window
Watching one little fly
Panicking wildly
Trying desperately to get out
Just that little fly
Reminds me of myself
Trapped somewhere it doesn't want to be
By something it cannot see.
My hand reaches out
Tugging gently at the latch of the window
I watch the poor thing rush
In a fluster it flies right out
Freed
Flying away to where it wants to be
How I wish it was me
From my glass cage set free.
Suddenly a sound pierces my ear
That darned bell snaps me back to reality
I realise I'm trapped by my glass cage
Until that wonderful time of home
Just like that little fly
I can float off to wherever I'm going
Away from here finally
Free!

Selina Thompson (14)
Cambridge House Grammar School

VISION OF YOU

Momentarily transfixed,
I move swiftly forward, reaching out,
Allowing myself to believe.
Fastening my gaze,
I explore your eyes,
Drinking in this moment,
Savouring your touch.
Shimmers of ecstasy encircle me,
Overpowering all innocent thoughts,
I'm enthralled, almost bewitched,
By your perfect posture,
Your capturing presence.
My vision of you, speaks of love.

Lyndsey Johnston (16)
Cambridge House Grammar School

TIME

Time has a way of turning castles into ruins
Time changes the most helpless child into the strongest man,
Time can change peace into war
And love into hate.

Time can change seeds into blossoming trees
Time changes joy into sadness
Time can heal the wounds we have
But it can also destroy our hopes.

Time, we know, is moving fast
But just how long will it be till the trumpet blasts?

Lauren Rock (16)
Cambridge House Grammar School

THE MIRACULOUS FOAL

I stood and watched in amazement
My first time seeing a foal being born
There she was, a golden chestnut colour
Standing in such pain
Her powerful legs give in to her
As she lies down, the foal starts to give way
Its dainty head all wet and graceful
Then the rest of its tiny body comes out with the afterbirth
Lying, protecting it
She cleans her foal and eats the afterbirth
After the foal is cleaned and dry he starts to try and get up
About half an hour later the foal is walking around with its mother
In the midday sun they then walk and stand under a shady tree.

Laura Kenny (15)
Cambridge House Grammar School

THE CHESTNUT HORSES

As the horse swiftly moved across
The grassy green field,
With wind blowing through her golden mane,
All was peaceful.
Her chestnut brown coat was silky
And shiny in the sun of the beautiful spring morning.
Her long, energetic legs slowed down
She lay down beside her foal
And they both were peaceful and content.

Kelly Orr (13)
Cambridge House Grammar School

THE END OF WINTER

When the winter evening settles down
And darkness wraps the landscape bleak,
Doors are closed and chimneys smoke,
The once crisp snow has melted to muddy slush.

The town now filled with darkness,
The street lamps reflect the icy footprints,
Where once the busy shoppers trod,
Trudging anxiously through the receding snow.

The scribbled February calendar page,
Is now followed by the clear spaced March,
A new month, a new season emerges,
Bringing hope of a bright new spring.

Sharon Reid (15)
Cambridge House Grammar School

PRELUDES

The winter evening settles down,
Snakes of traffic slowly tread
Upon the steely-frozen ground,
Streaked with light where the sun has bled.
Frost chokes the barren trees
And stills the sweet, crisp air,
Broken only by a few melancholy keys
Of the sullen wind's music that dares
To disturb the misty, silent sky.
The clouds start to cry.

Melissa Gordon (14)
Cambridge House Grammar School

EXAMS

Today I made the decision,
It would be wise to do some revision.
Parents and teachers nagging at me,
It will help, you'll see.

So when I got home I decided to revise,
I thought it would be wise
And I had a look,
At each subject revision book.

All these dates to learn for history,
Why it really is a mystery
And for English all those Shakespearean quotes,
There really are a lot of notes.

French and technology,
Maths and biology,
Chemistry and geography,
H_2O CO_2, Très bien and au revoir,
How will I ever cope?

However will I get them done,
When it takes a couple of hours, just to revise one,
It really is driving me mad,
But I hope I will do not too bad.

Scott Moore (14)
Cullybackey High School

AT NIGHT

Can she go to the grave?
Light
Not to be seen.

Animals I hear with fear
Impressive
Not.

Roaring goes the wind
Exaggerating
Why was it invented?

Claire Smyth (11)
Cullybackey High School

ALASTAIR

A lways slow
L ate for the bus
A lastair's mum has to fuss
S peed it up
T oe the line
A ny chance you could be on time
I 'm ready now
R elief all round.

Alastair Irvine (11)
Cullybackey High School

MICHAEL

M ischievous mixture
I ntelligent boy
C unning as a fox
H elpful and happy
A ctive and agreeable
E xciting and fantastic
L oopy and loony!

Michael Dickey (11)
Cullybackey High School

WHITE

The heavenly sight of falling snow
And sheep that look like cotton wool
I look high at the soft clouds in the sky
And can faintly hear angels singing
The scent of clean freshness
The innocence of a wedding day.

Charlene McFetridge (12)
Cullybackey High School

YELLOW

Bright, fluffy chicks tiptoeing about the yard.
Golden barley swaying in the breeze.
A blond-haired coward running away from danger.
An exercise book full from front to back.
A sweet sounding canary in its cage
And a fresh bunch of bananas ripening on their stalks.

David McCaughey (13)
Cullybackey High School

YELLOW

Sunflowers and daffodils swaying
in a summer breeze.
Playful chicks dancing in the field.
A happy feeling when you wake up
in the morning.
The glowing sun through the window.
Small birds singing in the sun.
The lovely sweet smell of primroses.

Janine Crawford (12)
Cullybackey High School

RAIN

Clear, blue, dull and grey
Trickling from the sky.

Smells like fresh, clean air
Gently floating by.

Drip, drop, splish, splash,
Like daggers on people's backs.

The sweet smell of pears
Makes your mouth water and smack.

Feels like a shower on your head
Soft, sprinkling, refreshing and clean.

Thank goodness for rain
Because it makes the grass green.

Patrick McCloskey (13)
Dunfane School

It Hurts To Be Alone

Loneliness fills my heart
Like a small child torn apart
I have no friends, no one
I do not play, I have no fun
My heart is throbbing
Inside I'm sobbing
But this remains hidden
Out of sight, from the forbidden.

Words cannot describe my thoughts
I know myself, I'm all I've got
I do not know, whom you may see
But I am the person I'm meant to be
Others, they may think, I seem alive
Though deep inside, I feel deprived
Let this hunger no longer grow
And hide this person full of woe
For it must stay disguised from the unknown
Who sympathise that lonely moan.

I'm smothering in this lonely field
But I'm protected from my smiling shield
Which prevents the ones who see
The quiet, aching, empty me.
I cannot bear it anymore
This powerful, silent, lonely sore.

Yes, words cannot describe my thoughts
For I am the only friend I've got.

Olivia Devlin (13)
St Louis Grammar School

IN THE FIELD

The morning sun begins to rise and lights this war-torn land,
The fighting didn't cease last night as I hoped and prayed it had,
The noise gets worse, the bombs they thud, soil rising to meet the sky,
O Lord why am I here, I know them not, yet I kill and am prepared to die.

I'm just eighteen, I know life not or what the future holds,
Yet here I am, gun in my hand, praying I will grow old,
I ask myself what quality of life will my comrades have?
Their arms and legs and sight now gone, the sacrifice for freedom
In our land.

I don't know why a brother has to take another's life,
What do we tell their loved ones, mothers, sisters, children, wife?
O yes, I'm me, I am the one who has caused you so much pain,
I took away your loved one and watched their blood dispersing
With the rain.

Please Lord let it be over soon I cannot take this anymore,
Bodies falling on the living, aching limbs, my heart so sore,
This cannot go on, who's responsible for this horrendous crime,
Man's inhumanity to man it seems will continue for all time.

But suddenly, the noise has ceased, the screaming and the yells,
I hear a deafening silence now and what a perfumed scented smell,
I know I felt the thud, a tear, but yet I heard no bang,
The bullet ripped straight through my heart and all the angels sang.

Marcus McCreight (13)
St Louis Grammar School

WAR

As I walked through the bleak battlefield
Full of hatred and deceit,
I dreamed contentedly,
Of who next I will defeat.

As the air fighters spun
Through the smoky singed air,
Bombs fell near,
But me, I did not care.

As the sick smell of death
Filled my senses,
Families tried to be brave,
But in reality, were defenceless.

One man fell to the ground
Due to opposition defences.
His body lay limp
Over the barbed wire fences.

Rats scuttled through the trenches,
Carrying disease and illness,
As men lay in fear
Of their enemies' willingness.

To banish them to Hell
With their loaded ammunition,
To wipe them out,
With great incision.

Clair McAllister (13)
St Louis Grammar School